THE MYTH
OF LEADERSHIP

THE MYTH
OF LEADERSHIP

CREATING
LEADERLESS
ORGANIZATIONS

JEFFREY S. NIELSEN

Davies-Black Publishing
Palo Alto, California

Published by Davies-Black Publishing, a division of CPP, Inc., 3803 East Bayshore Road, Palo Alto, CA 94303; 800-624-1765.

Special discounts on bulk quantities of Davies-Black books are available to corporations, professional associations, and other organizations. For details, contact the Director of Marketing and Sales at Davies-Black Publishing; 650-691-9123; fax 650-623-9271.

Visit the Davies-Black Publishing web site at www.daviesblack.com.

08 07 06 05 04   10 9 8 7 6 5 4 3 2 1
Printed in the United States of America

Library of Congress Cataloging-in-Publication Data
Nielsen, Jeffrey S.
    The myth of leadership : creating leaderless organizations / Jeffrey S. Nielsen.— 1st ed.
        p. cm.
    Includes bibliographical references and index.
    ISBN 0-89106-199-1 (hardcover)
    1. Leadership. 2. Organizational change. I. Title.

    HD57.7.N54 2004
    658.4′092—dc22
                                                            2003028301
FIRST EDITION
First printing 2004

To Doug and Kathy

Without pretense, they live what they believe and influence the world moment by moment.

CONTENTS

PREFACE

To grasp the contemporary issue and to meet its challenge calls for collective effort. It is not the individual but the group that transforms culture. —**Bernard Lonergan**

I have had the opportunity over the past seven years to travel to many different parts of the world talking to people about organizations. Whether it was civil servants in Washington, software programmers in London or Germany, telephone company employees in Israel, or undergraduate or graduate college students from all continents and many different countries, the vast majority have demonstrated their desire to make life in organizations meaningful, joyful, and prosperous. From the management executive to the frontline worker, these people possess the talent, competence, and motivation to make their organizations work. And yet, most organizations fail to live up to their expectations and fail to realize their potential.

In these conversations, I have observed the common barriers that block genuine organizational relationships and meaningful, dignified work. Individually, people possess the same basic values and desires, yet when they come together in organizations they become divided and opposed by these artificial barriers. Sadly, most of us make assumptions about our place and role in organizations that limit our and others' genuine opportunities for growth and development. In general, these assumptions involve the significance we place on leadership and the privileges we bestow on our leaders—frequently to the detriment of others in the organization. I call these beliefs, collectively, the *myth of leadership*.

Many people use the terms *leader* and *leadership* when trying to convey a sense of vision, of greater responsibility, of ownership over results, as well as greater productivity and more cohesive teamwork. What people often don't realize is that this concept and practice of leadership actually robs many individuals in organizations of the opportunity to contribute and share in these elements of organizational success. The purpose of this book is to challenge this myth of leadership and to introduce a model of organization that is fundamentally different from today's model of rank-based organization. I propose a radical new way of organizing and managing work and doing business—especially in the way people work together. The model makes the case for the end of leadership as we commonly know it— that is, rank-based management—and introduces a method for developing an organization into a true society of peers. I call this model the *peer-based organization.*

The peer-based organization is much more in harmony with organizational dynamics and the ever-increasing complexity of the business environment—as well as with our human aspirations, our basic needs and desires. It offers organizations a more efficient way to organize business and work relationships in a time of turbulent markets. It empowers employees to be more creative and gives them the motivation to think and act like owners. My intent is not based on morality or ethics; it is strategic—a peer-based organization will have competitive advantage over its rivals. It will be more successful. And yet it will also achieve the ethical goal of rehumanizing business and organizational life.

Today's corporate managers have been educated about the importance of teams and of finding new ways to lead that reject command-and-control managing. This book provides a methodology for putting those concepts into practice. Presented here are the assumptions, logic, and practices of both rank-based and peer-based organizational management and a template for transforming an organization from the former to the latter.

With the advent of the Internet and the World-Wide Web, I have been able to communicate with people all around the world who are expressing similar beliefs about and hopes for the project of creating peer-based organizations. A small number of people working toward the same goal in many different places and situations can begin to witness their small actions being amplified until they create a whole new understanding and a legacy of healthy, caring, more profitable organizations. I hope this book will move us in that direction, making the case that successful companies of the future will be leaderless, that is, peer-based, organizations.

ACKNOWLEDGMENTS

You will not do anything without others. —**Franz Kafka**

Writing a book is a daunting task, and it cannot be achieved alone. I need to thank those who have helped me along the way, first of all my family. Without their love, patience, and understanding, writing the book would have been more than daunting; it would have been impossible. My wife, Doreen, and my four children, Jill, Ryan, Rebecca, and Anna, have willingly sacrificed for many years to help make this book a reality. My mother and my late father, J. Larry Nielsen, have always served as an example to me of genuine love and concern. I should also mention Thorald and Lola Gene Rollins, who disprove all the negative stereotypes about in-laws.

I am thankful for my many colleagues, knowing people who exemplify goodness in their lives and who exhibit a real curiosity and desire for knowledge. I need to mention specifically Robert Crawford, Ed Donakey, Jeff Kearl, Stevie Keyes, Curt Porritt, Dennis Rasmussen, Buck Rose, Terry Warner, and Tenneson Woolf. I cannot forget the two ethics classes I taught at Brigham Young University in the spring and fall terms of 2003. These bright philosophy students helped me discover both the strengths and weaknesses in my understanding of peer-based organizations in our "Ethics of Leadership" course.

I also feel a deep gratitude for the following individuals for their encouragement, insights, friendship, and good conversation: Sterling Adams, Brent Barnett, Scott Hammond, Rob Hancock, Alexander Laszlo, Scott Pleune, Larry Ruff, Jeevan Sivasubramaniam, and Carl Zaiss. I would especially like to thank Rick Sidorowicz, editor of the online leadership journal *CEO Refresher* at refresher.com, for his support.

I began thinking about business and organizations as a graduate student in philosophy at Boston College. I was studying the brilliant Jesuit thinker Bernard Lonergan with a wonderful man, Joseph Flanagan. With Father Flanagan, I began to explore science—complexity and chaos theory—and human social organizations. From him I learned both a method of questioning and a process for learning. Pat Byrne, also of Boston College, and Ervin Laszlo, renowned systems thinker, have also been major intellectual influences. Though I do not quote these important twentieth-century thinkers at any length, their influence is everywhere present.

I am grateful to the entire team at Davies-Black Publishing for their wonderful dedication to improving organizational and individual life. My heartfelt thanks go especially to Connie Kallback for her vision of the possibilities of this project from the beginning. I am also grateful to Laura Simonds for her marketing talents and to Mark Chambers for his copyediting skill.

ABOUT THE AUTHOR

Jeffrey S. Nielsen, founder of Intellectual Capital Development, is passionate about working with organizations to develop peer-based leadership councils that awaken the productivity and creativity of the entire organization. He assists organizations in developing robust strategic business models that help them be creative, solve problems, and optimally adapt to their environment to create success. He specializes in strategic consulting and training to assist individuals in an organization learn how to act strategically, acquire knowledge-based skills that will not become obsolete, and begin to think like owners. To this end, he has created strategy, training, and organizational design models that give organizations the ability to transform challenges and crises in the environment for their gain and growth.

Nielsen is also a visiting lecturer at Brigham Young University, where he teaches "Ethics of Leadership." He formerly taught courses in ethics, reasoning and writing, and the history and development of science at Utah Valley State College. Prior to these appointments, he was a Teaching Fellow at Boston College, teaching courses in logic, critical thinking, and the history of science and art. He has also worked in financial services as a credit union legal representative and in community relations at Boston College, where he helped develop a mediation program for resolving student disputes and is currently completing a Ph.D. degree in philosophy. He received an undergraduate degree in German from Weber State College with an emphasis in economics.

Nielsen began his consulting and training career working with the Franklin Covey Company, where he presented workshops titled "Seven Habits of Highly Effective People" and "First Things First Time Management." He taught interpersonal communication workshops for special clients of the former Covey Leadership Center as well as overviews of Principle Centered Leadership. In this capacity he has traveled internationally, consulting with many Fortune 100 companies. He has also worked extensively with health care, computer, and information technology companies and frequently works with groups inside the federal government in Washington, D.C.

Nielsen has worked as well with the international outplacement and organizational consulting firm Right Management Consultants, Inc. His work there was primarily with human resource professionals and outplaced workers, and he helped HR professionals enhance their career service programs. His consulting work with downsized workers focused on coaching them in effective strategies to transition to new careers. He developed methods for individuals to assess their strengths and accomplishments, define their career objectives, and market themselves to potential employers. He specialized in training the job seeker in networking, interviewing, and negotiating skills and delivered change management and team-building workshops for Right Management both in the United States and in Europe.

For more information about creating peer-based organizations, or to learn about the competencies required to be successful in them, you can contact Nielsen at mythofleadership@hotmail.com.

PART ONE

THE CONTEXT
OF LEADERSHIP

CHAPTER 1

RANK-BASED VS. PEER-BASED THINKING IN ORGANIZATIONS

I felt first of all joyous. I felt that which joy is made of, and I realized that Joy itself must have been the impelling force, that which was there before we were there, and that somehow Joy was in every ingredient of our making. I think Joy is the key word in our work. It must be felt. If you don't feel Joy in what you're doing, then you are not really alive. **—Louis Kahn, architect**

Louis I. Kahn was one of our most innovative twentieth-century architects. Throughout his long career, he was always striving to help people find their place in the world; for him this was a joyous task. In a book that argues for creating space for the emergence of a new type of organization—a peer-based organization—I thought it fitting to open with a quote from a great builder of spaces. This, however, is not the only reason. Reading Kahn's writings and viewing his buildings have taught me that every practitioner of a discipline must find joy in creating. All visionaries, no matter their profession, have come to the same insight; namely, authentic human living is a joyful dialogue with the possibilities of being.

My particular interests are with the possibilities of business. Nowhere is it more important to find joy in creating than in the architecture of business space. You cannot make an organization unless you are joyously engaged — at least not one worth working in — just as working in a building that was not made joyously is itself a miserable thing. Designing, managing, and working in human organizations should be a joyous task. Whether you're an architect of a building, a business, or a life, your endeavor, to be personally meaningful, needs to be impelled by joy.

Today business is where the most influential ideas about human potential will be realized. Art Kleiner in *The Age of Heretics* (1996) says that "the purpose of a corporation is, and always has been, to re-create the world" (313). Yet how many of us involved in the creation, maintenance, and re-creation of organizational space find joy in this task? How many of us feel joyously engaged in re-creating our organization? How many of us experience joy working in our organization?

The current state of business does not allow the majority of individuals in corporations truly to enjoy their work. What needs to change so that all participants in business can experience a profitable increase in their own skills and competencies and bright futures in just and equitable organizations? What needs to change so that more people in these organizations will feel *impelled by joy* in their work?

TWO CRUCIAL OBSERVATIONS

Consulting with dozens of companies from every industry, I have made two observations you can take to the bank:

- Genuine communication occurs only between equals

- Secrecy frequently breeds corruption and abuse of power

In the absence of equality, you'll seldom have honest, open communication. You tell those above you only what you think they want to
hear, and you tell those beneath you only what you think they need
to know. This creates not only low levels of trust between individuals,
but a growing gap between business reality and the world of the top
executives, a gap that is endemic in almost every corporation today.

Similarly, with the lack of genuine communication, organizations
become obsessive about controlling access to information, and secrecy comes to dominate corporate life. With secrecy, positions of
power seduce even good people into taking undue advantage and
abusing their privileges. This is important to remember—even good,
decent people can get caught in this dynamic. It's not a character problem as much as a context problem. And the context, as I have come to
discover, is that of rank-based power and authority.

RANK-BASED LEADERSHIP

Robert Greenleaf (1996), one of the most thoughtful management
consultants of the twentieth century, recognized the danger inherent
in the rank-based nature of leadership, saying that "an important weak-
ness in the concept of the single chief at the top of a managerial
hierarchy is that such a person is apt to be a manager and to assume,
by virtue of having the position, that he or she has all of the talents
it requires" (101). Another great leader, Vaclav Havel (1994), who
came to political leadership as president of the Czech Republic when
it became democratic after the fall of the Soviet Union, said of rank
leadership:

*Again, being in power makes me permanently suspicious of
myself. What is more, I suddenly have a greater understanding
of those who are starting to lose their battle with the temptations
of power. In attempting to persuade themselves that they are still*

merely serving their [organization], they increasingly persuade themselves of nothing more than their own excellence, and begin to take their privileges for granted. (73)

If the rank-based context of leadership is a primary cause of unhealthy and joyless business organizations, it's time to start thinking about the possibility of organizations without rank. These organizations would be peer based as opposed to rank based. In rank-based organizations, a few people are elevated over the majority, who are subordinated to these few. In a peer-based organization, ranking simply wouldn't exist. Everyone would be considered to be of equal importance and worth, and personal involvement and mutual respect would lead to a sharing of responsibilities. In rank-based organizations, those lower in the company are frequently sacrificed for the benefit of those higher in the company. In peer-based organizations, all employees would be seen as playing an equally important role—where what benefits one should benefit all, and what hurts one will hurt all. Leadership, I realized, is by definition a rank-based concept.

Even such appealing conceptions of leadership as Robert Greenleaf's "servant leadership" imply ranking, division, and separation. Whenever we think in terms of "leadership," we create a dichotomy: (1) leaders, a select and privileged few, and (2) followers, the vast majority. There follows the implicit judgment that leaders are somehow superior to followers. So you get secrecy, distrust, overindulgence, and the inevitable sacrifice of those below for the benefit of those above. The word *leadership*, in fact, immediately creates a ranked division of people in ways that do not serve healthy organizational relationships. It also produces a privileged elite who, no matter how sincere they are, will eventually be seduced by their position. That's why I argue for creating peer-based organizations. And a peer-based organization would essentially be a leaderless organization.

THE PEER-BASED ALTERNATIVE

When you work with a peer, do you consider yourself the leader and the other person the follower? Or, do you believe that the other person is the leader, and you are the follower? No, there is really no thought of leadership because there is no thought of ranking. The word *peer* does not create separate categories—it is a holistic notion, where a diversity of talents and abilities is recognized within the idea of equality of worth and value. With peer-based organizations, we can achieve unity in diversity and diversity in unity. A good friend, Sterling Adams, suggested that this is what happens in a pickup game of football.

Playing with Peers

I had only recently participated in my family's traditional "Turkey Bowl" over the Thanksgiving holiday. My son, brothers, cousins, uncles, and I self-organized into two teams and played a rowdy game of touch football. There was no "boss," but depending on our comparative talents, we volunteered to begin playing the different positions with the shared purpose of helping our team win. In the huddle, there was no official lead play caller, but we all suggested what might work given our experience of the previous play. We came to consensus quite quickly, and almost always rotated positions so everyone had a turn at quarterback, receiver, and lineman. The team really was, in miniature, a society of peers. These games are always fiercely competitive, and no one enjoys losing, but rank is not even a consideration. On those rare occasions when we invite someone new to play, and that person considers himself better than the rest of the team and so entitled to take over and dominate the game, the members of this unlucky team tend to quickly lose interest and try to finish the game as soon as possible.

Of course, we make sure that person is not invited back the following year.

Winning Decisions

With this experience in mind, we enjoy two key insights in "playing" with peers that relate to my earlier observations. First, it is important for success that decisions be made by those closest to where the real work is being done. (In fact, the case could be made for defining the leader as the person doing the actual work.) That doesn't happen in an organization that's secretive and protective of information and power. For instance, in our pickup game there was one play where I was at quarterback, and I wanted to send Ryan, the wide receiver, on a quick passing route. He recommended, instead, a long bomb, knowing what I didn't know: namely, that the man defending him was rather slow. Ryan knew he could easily run past him. I deferred the decision to him, and we subsequently scored a touchdown on the long pass.

Genuine Communication

This leads to the second key insight: Genuine communication will only occur between peers. Had Ryan not believed we were working together on this team as peers, he would not have made the suggestion he did, I would not have yielded the decision to him, and we would not have scored a touchdown. On those unfortunate, yet thankfully rare, occasions when I have played with someone who thought he was my superior, and everyone else's, none of us "inferior" players offered suggestions. We refused any responsibility and ceded all the play calling to the dominator, no matter how lousy it was, and told him what he wanted to hear. We learned quickly that only by gaining his approval did we have a chance that he would pass the ball to us.

An Organizational Ball Hog

I was reminded of this type of "ball hog" when I was consulting with a high-tech company in London. I was trying to help them organize a decision-making process that would gather input from all the employees, when I encountered stiff resistance from the senior executive. He bluntly informed me that employees should have no influence on the direction or decisions of the company. They were, he told me, as if imparting some esoteric management knowledge, "meant to be used like light bulbs: you screw 'em in, you turn 'em on, you burn 'em out. Then you replace 'em." I did not find even one of this executive's direct reports who found his or her work in this company to be either joyful or meaningful, and I held numerous private conversations with these reports in a four-month period. Yet no leader—not just an arrogant leader like this one—can escape the damage to relationships in a rank-based organization. Even the most benign and open-minded leaders will in the end create dependence and compliance in their direct reports, not interdependence and commitment.

RANK-BASED THINKING

I discovered one of the most generous and well-intentioned leaders I have ever known while consulting with a telecommunications company in Tel Aviv. This man sincerely wanted his people to feel empowered to do their job and to work together as a team. He spent a lot of money giving them the training and tools they would need to be more proactive and cooperative at work. He also genuinely wanted their honest feedback about his effectiveness as a leader. Yet he was still the boss, and while he wanted their input, he retained control over decision making. So, even though he sought their honest and genuine communication, they told him what they thought he wanted to hear:

pleasant lies. And even though he wanted them to take initiative and be proactive, they remained dependent and merely compliant to the established procedures of the hierarchic, rank-based organization. The irony here is obvious, yet this type of misunderstanding is the norm where categories of "leader" and "follower" exist. With rank-based thinking, a gap grows between the decision maker at the top and reality at the front line, no matter how genuine and sincere the leader.

Collaboration and consensus building, not command and control, are the most effective strategies for increasing productivity, decreasing costs, promoting creative problem solving, and improving quality in organizations. Yet collaboration and consensus building are difficult when the organization is weighted down with rank-based thinking. There have been many excellent new ideas in management thinking over the past two decades, but I believe their true value has been minimized by the absence of peer-based relationships. Only in the space of peer-based thinking can the important disciplines, habits, and emotional intelligence come to full maturity.

PEER-BASED THINKING

Peer-based thinking allows everyone to find their unique talents and make their authentic contribution to create a stronger organization than ever thought possible. It does not reduce everyone to sameness, for in peer-based organizations there will not necessarily be equal talents, or equal outcomes, or even equal opportunities, but there will be equal standing with an openness that invites individuals to find their own level and degree of contribution. Already there are organizations that realize there is more intelligence and energy in an organization of peers than in an organization that values only the top few. Four such successful, peer-based, nearly leaderless organizations (discussed in greater detail later in the book) are listed here:

1. Semco, a company based in São Paulo, Brazil, is mentored by its maverick owner, Ricardo Semler. It has been consistently profitable in a country with one of the most unstable governments and highly inflationary economies in the world.

2. The Orpheus Chamber Orchestra in Manhattan is internationally recognized and Grammy nominated. Since its inception in 1970, this world-class orchestra has worked without a conductor.[1]

3. W. L. Gore & Associates, in Newark, Delaware, is a chemical engineering and product manufacturing company famous for its lack of assigned leaders and managers.

4. Motek, in Beverly Hills, California, is a vibrant company that develops supply chain execution software solutions for warehousing and distribution companies.

All four of these organizations have realized that to access and unleash its inherent intelligence and energy, an organization must adopt new management thinking contrary to ranking.

RANK-BASED VS. PEER-BASED ORGANIZATIONS

Obviously, an organization designed to be peer based will be very different from its rank-based counterpart. Rank-based thinking suppresses the heart and intelligence of the majority of an organization's employees. Command-and-control managing under the influence of rank-based thinking tends to be harsh, coercive, and demotivating. It is

1. Executive Director Harvey Seifter and Peter Economy wrote a book detailing the journey entitled *Leadership Ensemble: Lessons in Collaborative Management from the World's Only Conductorless Orchestra* (New York: Times Books, 2001).

likely to create a poisonous atmosphere in the organization that kills an employee's natural desire to cooperate and be productive. Peer-based thinking rejects rank and supports a different type of organization, one that respects all members of the organization as peers.

The very form of peer-based organizations promotes the heart and intelligence of all employees. The more individual employees participate in decision making, the more their energy and dedication are enlisted by the organization. Allowed to share in business deliberations, individual employees expand their range of concerns beyond narrow self-interest to include a disciplined concern for the well-being of the whole organization. Most rank-based companies discourage the average individual's participation in decision making.

Deprived of a share in business deliberations, individual employees become almost totally absorbed with their own individual concerns and needs. Many rank-based leaders view this as further proof of their need to control decision making. They are blind to how rank-based leadership by nature creates self-centered employees. Thomas Kuhn (1962) said we don't see something until we have the right metaphor to let us perceive it. Most of our mental models, particularly in business, are still rank based. We need a new gestalt.

John Case (1993), in a cover story for *Inc.* magazine, pointed out that "a twenty-first century company's task will be to organize work so it can be carried out by businesspeople—by men and women who take responsibility and who share in the risks and rewards of enterprise" (93). Ten years later, most companies still have not created this sort of organization. I believe a main reason for this failure is the absence of a proper understanding of rank-based versus peer-based thinking. When a leader tries to share decision-making responsibility with others but fails to address the underlying rank-based thinking, any positive results will be short-term. The long-term results will include an increase in employee cynicism and an increase in rank-based control.

DANGERS IN NOT CHALLENGING
RANK-BASED THINKING

In consulting with and training hundreds of employees with dozens of different organizations, I've discovered a real desire on the part of the employees to make significant contributions. We all share a desire to make contributions and be recognized for them. We all desire to feel self-worth. Many organizations are structured to make this nearly impossible. Yet from time to time a leader in a rank-based organization comes along who wants to challenge the status quo and allow greater participation from the ranks below. This can have drastic and immediate positive effects on the company, but those beneficial results will fade if the underlying paradigm of rank-based thinking is not addressed and replaced with peer-based thinking. A good example is merchandise retailer Sears, Roebuck & Company during the 1990s.

Rank-Based Thinking at Sears

In 1992, Sears had a financial loss of $3.9 billion and was faced with the real possibility of still worsening business conditions. The CEO at the time did everything in his power to turn things around. It was, however, an attempt at top-down damage control. As recounted by authors Pascale, Millemann, and Gioja in *Surfing the Edge of Chaos: The Laws of Nature and the New Laws of Business* (2000), "One regional manager characterizes the atmosphere as one of 'salute-and-obey.' Directives came down from above and we did our best to follow them" (46). This type of rank-based solution only allowed the situation to grow worse as both employee morale and customer satisfaction decreased. It was time for a change of leadership.

Peer-Based Thinking at Sears

The new CEO brought in was Arthur C. Martinez. Martinez took many actions to correct the downward slide of Sears, which in most cases involved shifting the power of decision making and control to frontline employees. Martinez developed what were called the "3 Cs," or the three "compellings": a compelling place to shop, a compelling place to work, and a compelling place to invest. This opened up Sears to incredible employee-based initiative and innovation. Empowering the employees had the obvious consequence of boosting employee job satisfaction. What wasn't expected was how higher employee job satisfaction directly led to higher customer satisfaction. As Pascale, Millemann, and Gioja point out, Martinez was able to exactly quantify this increase. "The evaluation demonstrated that a 5 percent improvement in employee satisfaction caused a 1.3 percent improvement in customer satisfaction" (52). The 1.3 percent jump in customer satisfaction also led to an 0.5 percent increase in store revenue.

By 1995, Martinez, with these peer-based initiatives, seemed to have turned Sears around. Not only were profitability and the share price back up, but Sears was also recognized as one of the most admired companies as measured by employee satisfaction. In 1997, *Fortune* named Sears "the most innovative general merchandise retailer." The future looked bright. Unfortunately, Martinez had never adequately challenged the rank-based thinking of his senior executives. He had turned the rank-and-file employees loose to innovate and speak up, but all under the suspicious gaze of other senior leaders.

Reversion to Rank-Based Thinking at Sears

When difficult financial decisions had to be made, some senior executives took it upon themselves to impose them from above in classic command-and-control style. Rank-based leadership habits are hard to break. For all of Martinez' peer-based thinking, senior leadership remained rank based, and they waited for their opportunity to reexert control. Already by the end of the 1990s these rank-based leaders were making it difficult for Martinez' more peer-based initiatives. When he left Sears in 2001, the retailer reverted to rank-based thinking with predictable consequences. In late 2002, the retailer warned that it would miss its third-quarter earnings estimates, and the stock dropped more than 14 percent—its biggest one-day drop in fifteen years. The company's 2003 results were poor.

It's not enough to institute peer-based behaviors in an organization without explicitly addressing the paradigm of rank-based thinking. Most employees want a part in the decision making and managing of work in their organization. In fact, the measure of control employees have over their work is a good indicator of their overall job satisfaction. It is a drastic blow to employee morale when one leader gives them control and, just as quickly, another leader takes it away. That leaders have the right to command over others whose chief duty is to obey is engrained in our thinking, especially among those who achieve the leadership position. Only by explicitly challenging this rank-based thinking can it be changed.

CONCLUSION

For most of us, life evolves around our job in an organization, so it is important to make that job meaningful, dignified, and joyful. Creating and designing organizations in a way that fosters creativity and cooperation should be everyone's top priority. In our most optimistic dreams, our job in an organization can be one where we say to our neighbor, "You are my peer. You are my equal." We can realize that the only boundaries and barriers that separate us are artificial. For our children and children's children, let this be the generation that transcends these artificial limits and creates joyful and just communities of peers. This is not just a hopeful ideal, but a necessity for those companies that want to have ongoing and long-term prosperity in the coming business environment.

Peer-based thinking builds better, more healthy and prosperous organizations than does rank-based thinking, which creates an organizational culture where people

- Withhold important information and valuable resources

- Try to control others

- Blame others

Organizations need to create a culture where everyone desires, and is able, to do their best to achieve outstanding results for the company. Of course, this would be a peer-based organization. This is a new concept for most people, and it seems so radically different from what most of us have ever experienced. Why should we even believe that an organization can be run effectively without rank-based leaders? Responding to this legitimate concern requires, I believe, that we first examine how we have come to understand leadership. In chapters 2 and 3 we will see that our concept of leadership has been a function of our history, not an expression of our remarkable, yet mostly unexplored, human potential.

CHAPTER 2

THE MYTH OF LEADERSHIP

At the head of the table ... was an old man. His napkin was tied around his neck like a child's. ... This was the marquis's father-in-law, the old duc de Laverdière ... said to have been Marie-Antoinette's lover ... he led a wild, dissipated life, filled with duels, wagers and abductions; he had ... been the terror of his family. ... Emma's eyes kept coming back to ... [him] as though he were ... august. He had lived at court! He had slept with a queen! —**Gustave Flaubert,** *Madame Bovary*

In Gustave Flaubert's novel *Madame Bovary* (1949), the heroine, Emma, is star-struck in the presence of the ranked class, the aristocracy. She is especially captivated by the old duc de Laverdière. In her mind, this decayed man is the epitome of greatness. She sees a dashing, gallant man of action and romance, while the reader sees the reality of a worn-out, dilapidated, empty shell of a man, whose life is no more gallant and dashing than the gravy dripping from his unhealthy, oversized lips. The contrast is striking, and I couldn't help but begin this chapter on the myth of leadership with this arresting image from Flaubert. The old aristocrat could very well be the poster child for leadership—or more precisely, for the myth of leadership—where rank alone demands and generally gets awe and respect, not to mention grand rewards. Emma's unfortunate life will play itself out through her distorted perception of reality, blinded by the false glow of superior rank. Every day in business, similar tragedies play themselves out—as employees and managers fall victim to the rank-based myth of leadership.

EXPOSING THE MYTH

I use as my definition of *myth* one supplied by James Robertson in his *American Myth, American Reality* (1980):

> Myths are "the way things are" as people in a particular society believe them to be; and they are the models people refer to when they try to understand their world, and its behavior. Myths are the patterns of behavior, of belief, and of perception, which people have in common. Myths are not deliberately, or necessarily consciously, fictitious. (xv)

The myth of leadership plays to our human disposition to see history as a series of dramatic events involving only a few heroic, gifted individuals. It is much easier to account for things this way. To see events as a consequence of a single heroic person is less intellectually challenging than to see them as the consequence of many different factors and the subtle influence of small acts. When we view history this way, however, we tend to overlook and devalue the impact of the vast majority of people who lack status but who truly contribute to making things work.

The myth of leadership governing organizational life today sustains the belief that only the relatively few "gifted" ones can be anointed leaders in an organization and so trusted to make the decisions and do the commanding and controlling of everyone else. But we all desire to make significant contributions, to feel self-worth, to be recognized for what we do—and many organizations are structured to make this nearly impossible. Every management act and decision follows from assumptions, generalizations, and hypotheses, frequently subconscious, concerning human nature and human behavior, setting the stage for how we design, organize, and run companies. Rarely do leaders question these assumptions, or think about where they might have picked them up, but rather are inclined to think that this is just the way people are.

These rank-based assumptions rob too many employees of self-worth and create irresolvable tensions for others. The myth is therefore a brake on the natural evolution and success of business organizations as well as a hindrance to the enjoyment of a meaningful life in business institutions. It makes business and other organizations much less productive than they could be, as the real talents of too many employees are never developed or used. Rejecting the myth, I believe, will pave the way for more open organizations to foster greater value and joy in our working lives.

The Celebrity CEO

A company's success is generally attributed to the actions of its chief executive (most likely a man). But all too often a chief executive leaves a successful company to replicate that success at a different company, but then turns out to be a flop. Too bad for him, we think—he must have lost his touch. Of course, the real reason is that he never had it in the first place. With the first company he got lucky and was there when the market dynamics were in his favor. At the next company, he bought into the idea of his own genius—the myth-of-leadership mentality—and trusting only his own wisdom, made decisions that probably went against the dynamic and created a failure. Today the majority of successful "leaders" are lucky rather than good. The myth of leadership keeps us from understanding this.

RANK-BASED VS. PEER-BASED LEADERSHIP ASSUMPTIONS

To understand the power and durability of the myth of leadership—why it has such a strong hold on our imagination—we need to examine its assumptions about leaders and followers. We must begin by recognizing that these assumptions are not absolute, universal truths—they have a history. This history has helped establish the now implicit justification and legitimization of our current rank-based notion of leadership.

Three events, beginning in the seventeenth century and maturing in the nineteenth century, have contributed to the acceptance of the myth in modern organizations:

- The triumph of Newtonian science and its accompanying world-view

- The understanding of human nature inherent in Enlightenment philosophies

- The reaction to Enlightenment rationalism in Romanticism, creating the modern concept of individual genius and celebrity

Each of these events has worked its way into modern business assumptions about leaders and followers, affecting the way we organize work and relationships. They have led to rank-based organizations that overestimate the senior executive and underestimate the rank-and-file employee. They have introduced rank-based thinking into business in a way that makes work less than meaningful for the majority of individuals involved. Table 1 outlines some of these rank-based assumptions

TABLE 1: RANK- VS. PEER-BASED ASSUMPTIONS	
Rank-Based Assumptions	**Peer-Based Assumptions**
Employees are lazy	Employees are productive
Employees are selfish	Employees are caring
Leaders are heroic individuals	Each individual is unique
Leadership command and control	General input and participation
Knowledge at the top	Knowledge at all levels
Manipulation	Cooperation

and contrasts them with peer-based assumptions that can lead to more successful relationships and more successful organizations. We will discuss each of these contrasts in detail.

Employees Are Lazy vs. Employees Are Productive

The influence of science on business is a key factor in our first rank-based assumption.

Rank-Based Assumption
Employees are by nature lazy and need external motivation.

Peer-Based Assumption
Employees tend to be productive and self-motivated.

In most business organizations, employees are treated as costs that have to be justified. They are just parts, expensive parts, of the machine of business that must be operated as cheaply as possible. Where did this view of individual employees originate? Most organizational theorists agree it was in science, specifically Newtonian science. Newton introduced the most comprehensive and powerful explanation of how natural systems behave the way they do. His fellow scientists wept when they read his *Mathematical Principles of Natural Philosophy* (1687), thinking that it was now all over, that there was nothing great left to discover. He "proved" that systems were composed of bodies, and those bodies were governed by basic forces. Bodies were inert and would change course only if acted upon by these basic forces. His system of natural science soon shaped the way we viewed human systems, organizations, work, and hence the leadership of work performed in organizations.

Newton's model seemed to justify its imitation in all fields of human endeavor, including management science. Just as nature had been mechanized and reduced to nothing but bodies in motion, labor was thought to be nothing but bodies in motion that had to be coerced through external force. Without an outside push or pull, the "Newtonian" employee would remain inert; that is, lazy and unmotivated. Frederick W. Taylor was the chief promoter and practitioner of this view, albeit motivated by socially admirable goals. His time and motion studies reveal the belief that a rigorous mechanical approach to organizations would bring superb results in the scientific management of workers.

Taylor believed that leadership must be imposed from the top down in a command-and-control manner. The brains and intelligence of a company resided at the top, while the muscle for doing the actual work resided at the bottom. He made two critical assumptions: (1) brain work should be taken from the shop floor and placed in the executive office, and (2) management should take all relevant knowledge and reduce it to rules, formulas, and laws for the rank and file to mindlessly follow.

In this system, employees were reduced to machines competing for scarce goods with other similar, yet separate, machines in an alien and often hostile workplace. This mentality was soon applied to organizations, people, and the environment without differentiation by the new scientific business leaders, not all of whom, by the way, shared Taylor's high ideals. They believed that to motivate they must push or prod a worker into action, overcoming the worker's inertia by the sheer force of their own bullying. For this, they found complete justification in science.

Now there is general agreement that the understanding of the nature of reality in classical science is not only wrong with regard to the natural world, but is detrimental to organizations as well. The majority of processes and systems found in nature cannot be reduced to nothing more than the behavior of inert bodies in motion. Similarly, employees are not machines, but living, open systems capable of self-renewal and self-direction. While natural science, with its self-correcting method, has moved beyond this limiting belief about natural systems, management science has all too frequently remained bound to this inaccurate assumption about human systems. Today the belief that employees tend to be lazy and require external motivation is part of the unconscious fabric of leadership thought and practice. It creates a self-fulfilling prophecy, where seeing employees as lazy and unmotivated creates an organizational culture where the employees become lazy and unmotivated.

When managers treat their employees as unmotivated "cost centers" who require constant supervision, employees become defensive and respond by doing the bare minimum to avoid making mistakes or standing out. It doesn't take long for an employee who started out with great enthusiasm to become dependent on the rank-based leader's management of all important decisions, until soon the employee loses all initiative. New hires in a rank-based organization come to work full of innovative ideas and energy only to retreat into a compliant "just doing what I'm told" mentality after repeatedly being put in their place by some threatened rank-based manager.

Employees Are Selfish vs. Employees Are Caring

The second rank-based assumption finds its roots in the nature of the individual as described in the writings of Enlightenment philosophers such as Thomas Hobbes.

Rank-Based Assumption
Employees are by nature selfish and self-seeking and therefore need external control to keep them in line.

Peer-Based Assumption
Employees tend to be caring and willing to cooperate.

Hobbes argued that individuals are naturally in constant anxiety motivated by two basic emotions: (1) a negative emotion, the fear of death, and (2) a positive emotion, desire for all material goods and the domination of others. These two motivations put us into constant agitation with an insatiable craving for material wealth and, at the same time, a fear of death in a world that will not satisfy our infinite wants and constantly threatens to destroy us as well. In this world only the paranoid survive. As autonomous individuals constantly responding to these two emotions, individuals are in a state of a constant war of everyone against everyone. As Hobbes (1982) pointed out, in this environment, "life is poor, nasty, brutish, and short" (92).

Hobbes, like most Enlightenment philosophers, wanted to discover how and why individuals join together in organizations. Organizations will only come into existence, he argued, if autonomous individuals consent to organize for their own protection against each other and thus sacrifice certain freedoms to the organization and whoever controls it. In this view, individuals give up much of their freedom and enter organizations via common agreement (the social contract) in order to escape their natural wretched condition. Even as they enter organizations, they still retain their basic motivating emotions of fear of death as well as the insatiable desire for material goods. The purpose of any organization, in this view, is one of protecting people from each other as each struggles to acquire as much wealth and power as possible. (Certainly, this is a view of organizations expected and favored by market analysts.) These assumptions place the individual in constant opposition to others in the organization. They permeate through all our organizational thinking, planning, and communication, leading to the all-pervasive us-versus-them thinking that poisons relations between the company and its employees, or management and labor.

Us vs. Them

No one has captured the ironic nature of this conflict better than the writer Franz Kafka. He depicts the perplexed individual trapped in a maze not of his own making—the more he struggles, the more entrapped he becomes. The protagonist in my favorite Kafka story, *The Metamorphosis* (1915), is a young office worker by the name of Gregor Samsa, who wakes up one morning after unsettling dreams to discover he has turned into a dung beetle! Stuck on his back, unable to move, he fails to make it to work for the first time in his career. Gregor has been the ever-faithful employee even though trapped in a menial and boring job. He has accepted his fate while never once coming to work late. But guess who shows up rather quickly to evaluate the situation? It's none other than his manager, who immediately casts suspicion on his honesty and work ethic.

> *"Mr. Samsa," the manager now called, raising his voice, "what's the matter? You barricade yourself in your room, answer only 'yes' and 'no,' cause your parents serious, unnecessary worry, and you neglect—I mention this only in passing—your duties to the*

firm in a really shocking manner. . . . The head of the firm did
suggest to me this morning a possible explanation for your tardi-
ness—it concerned the cash payments recently entrusted to
you—but really, I practically gave my word of honor that the
explanation could not be right. But now, seeing your incompre-
hensible obstinacy, I am about to lose even the slightest desire to
stick up for you in any way at all. . . . Your performance of late
has been very unsatisfactory; I know it is not the best season for
doing business, we all recognize that; but a season for not doing
any business, there is no such thing. Mr. Samsa, such a thing
cannot be tolerated." (Kafka 1981, 99)

In this passage we see the first two assumptions of the myth of leadership: (1) employees are naturally lazy, and (2) they are naturally
prone to dishonesty and self-seeking behavior—even to theft against
the employer. Kafka's antiheroes are always getting caught in the
absurdity of command-and-control hierarchies that threaten their well-
being for seemingly trivial reasons. Here, with the anonymous and
unpredictable power the manager and head of the firm hold over
Gregor's head, his fear of failure is heightened. Today, with almost
constant layoffs and restructuring, which seldom actually improve
organizations, this nameless and capricious power held by leaders over
their followers is incredibly harmful to our social fabric.

The Desire to Make a Difference

A rank-based organization informed by the myth of leadership tends to
limit the creativity of employees to the narrow confines of their job
description. What these rank-based assumptions overlook is that most
people work for a broader reward, including at least the following three
things:

- Fair compensation
- A chance to develop skills and new talents
- The opportunity to contribute to a cause larger than themselves

Employees bring their whole person to work, but the rank-based organization seeks to limit their involvement to impersonal tasks. This tension between individuals as whole persons and the limited organizational role assigned them often leads to employees just putting in their time at work before getting to do what's really meaningful for them after work. This doesn't have to be, for most employees seek first to find meaning and value at work, but it is too often denied them.

Leaders Are Heroic Individuals vs. Each Individual Is Unique

The third rank-based assumption has given the leadership myth its potent emotional appeal.

Rank-Based Assumption

Leaders are heroic individuals who have risen above the masses—possessing either an innate or learned genius. They are better than those beneath them, thus have the right to control decision making in organizations and do all the commanding and controlling.

Peer-Based Assumption

Leaders are no different than employees—they each have their own unique strengths and weaknesses.

I once worked with a leader who had quickly climbed to the top of his organization. When we first talked soon after his promotion, he was anxious to tell me he wasn't surprised by his meteoric rise, "for the cream will always rise to the top." This, I believe, captures an essential part of the leadership myth, namely, that those at the top of the organization are somehow better, or more deserving, than those beneath them on the organizational chart. What are the roots of this conception?

The Renaissance saw the rise in the fame of artists, but it was Romanticism, with its belief in creative genius and the romantic hero, that gave birth to personality cults and the appeal of the leadership myth of the twentieth century. From Romanticism we get our idea of the superhero, the master-of-the-universe type, who single-handedly controls others and the elements to achieve his desires and set the course of history.

Two books on the subject, both of which were tremendously popular when published, were pivotal. One is a series of lectures by Thomas Carlyle published in 1841 as *On Heroes, Hero-Worship, and the Heroic in History*. The other, published in 1850 by Carlyle's friend and correspondence partner Ralph Waldo Emerson, is entitled *Representative Man*. Both books promote the greatness in men and provide the arguments for the importance and presence of "great men" in society and business. Carlyle wrote:

> *We ... discourse here ... on Great Men, their manner of appearance in our world's business, how they have shaped themselves in the world's history, what I call Hero-worship and the Heroic in human affairs. ... A large topic; indeed, an illimitable one; wide as Universal History itself. For, as I take it, Universal History, the history of what man has accomplished in this world, is at bottom the History of the Great Men who have worked here. They were the leaders of men, these great ones; the modelers, patterns, and in a wide sense creators, of whatsoever the general mass of men contrived to do or to attain; all things that we see standing accomplished in the world are properly the outer material result, the practical realization and embodiment, of Thoughts that dwelt in the Great Men sent into the world.* (1)

If you believe, following Newtonian science, that the majority of people are by nature lazy and need external force to motivate them—and if you believe, from the selfish individualism of Hobbes, that people will give up their freedom and join organizations because they are coerced and controlled by their own or others' self-seeking fear and greed—it is an easy step to assume that it could only be through the heroic efforts of some creative genius, a *leader*, that such an organization could be established and made successful. This "Great Man" (or today, perhaps "Great Woman") has, through his own wit, work, and luck, climbed to the top, assumed his destiny as the leader, and can now benefit the organization. His position at the top enables him to reap huge rewards, command large organizations, and demand that others give up their freedom to his judgment.

Of course, the reality of this heroic leader frequently resembles the "emperor's new clothes." The executive I mentioned earlier, who quickly climbed to the top of his organization, was not respected by those beneath him in rank. As I learned more about him and his successes, I discovered that he often claimed credit when others had done the work. I also found out that many of the contracts and partnership deals he arranged in his quick rise were poorly structured and fell apart soon after he was promoted to his next leadership position. The senior executives had so thoroughly bought into the assumptions of the myth of leadership, however, that these failings were blamed on his replacements, and his image remained untarnished.

Leadership Command and Control vs. General Input and Participation

The fourth rank-based assumption is that the corporate leader, as hero, must also have nearly superhuman capabilities.

Rank-Based Assumption

The heroic leader can control a complex organization from the top down, can accurately predict what is going to happen in the future, and should therefore be making all the critical decisions.

Peer-Based Assumption

Only with input and participation from all levels of the organization can leaders make effective decisions about current and future business conditions.

This leader becomes the indispensable avenue for every significant action in the organization; indeed, it wouldn't happen without her. Such a leader will be suspicious of, and unwilling to delegate any important decision to, anyone who does not see things her way. As a leader, she of course has vision, and those who follow her will be on the front wave of future success. Those who disagree with her vision, or, if they're without vision, will not progress within the leader's organization. In this view, decisions can be made only by the leader and not by the mass of people in the organization, who cannot be trusted to share the genius of the leader.

This rank-based assumption not only keeps decision making at the top of the organization—thus robbing the organization of the intelligence and talents of the vast majority of employees—it also corrupts communication. A rank-based leader will see his position as more important than the positions of those lower in rank. Because of this perception of superiority, the leader will not seek input or, if it is given, not take seriously the input of someone lower in rank.

This view of genius in eighteenth- and nineteenth-century Romanticism merged with Hobbes's belief in the nature of the individual, and the belief in how they interact from Newtonian science, and created the myth of leadership in twentieth-century organizations to justify rank-based forms of social arrangements. It is a belief that must be constantly justified in organizations. The justification is enforced through the tight control of information via closed books and closed meetings; through the media's obsession with celebrity and emphasis on leaders as larger-than-life individuals; and through the plethora of popular books on leadership.

Knowledge at the Top vs. Knowledge at All Levels

In the fifth rank-based assumption, knowledge and understanding are also considered to be the domain of the few.

Rank-Based Assumption
Employees tend not to know the best thing to do, while leaders do know.

Peer-Based Assumption
Individuals closest to where the work is done have a good grasp on what needs to happen.

Numerous books on leadership promise to reveal the leadership secrets of Attila the Hun, Moses, or Abraham Lincoln, or even Jesus as a CEO. They attempt to justify an implicit theory of motivation and human nature where only a few great individuals can lead—and if you want to lead, you have to be just like them. Not surprisingly, it is also a theory that tends to reward only a few with tremendous benefits in salaries and other bonuses; for if it takes superhuman abilities to lead, then it also requires superhuman salaries to reward these few "Great Men." So, the myth in many ways justifies the great disparity between salaries paid to senior executives and the wages of the majority of people in organizations. It certainly helps drive executives' compensation way out of proportion to their actual worth to organizations.

In fact, some recent studies show an inverse relationship between executive compensation and profit performance of the company. A report issued by Scott Klinger (2001) of United for a Fair Economy showed that over half the companies in the top 10 percent in executive pay had a stock price that underperformed the S&P 500. In addition to the poor profit and stock performance, companies with the highest paid CEOs were more likely to announce significant layoffs within three years of their CEO appearing on the top paid list. An interesting aspect to exorbitant executive pay is that if minimum wage had increased at the same rate as executive pay since 1990, which was at a rate of 571 percent, then it would be not $5.15 an hour, but $25.50 an hour.

More often than not, celebrity CEOs are a product of their organization and not its cause. Very few find similar success when they go somewhere else, though they do pull in quite substantial compensation packages. Not surprisingly, the myth is supported by those who have been anointed leaders as well as by those who would like to be anointed leaders and reap the huge monetary and social rewards.

Paradoxically, our present myth of leadership, which arose from currents of thought that stressed individualism and individual greatness, has resulted in organizational managers turning into carbon copies of one another. In the words of Edward Young (1683–1765), "Born originals how comes it to be that we die as copies?" Further, what Vaclav Havel (1994) observed about political leaders could be said as well for CEOs of organizations:

> *He becomes a captive of his position, his perks, his office. What apparently confirms his identity and thus his existence in fact subtly takes that identity and existence away from him. He is no longer in control of himself, because he is controlled by something else: his position and its exigencies, its consequences, its aspects, and its privileges.* (73–74)

The myth of leadership also creates several mistaken assumptions about ways to motivate employees. For instance, many leaders assume that the chief way to motivate employees is to give them more money. However, research conducted by Fred Emery has shown that money, while a work satisfier, is not a work motivator (Weisbord 1991, 167–168). Understanding the difference between work motivators and work satisfiers is important in creating a successful organization. What will motivate employees is to give them greater control and influence over their work; however, this is something a leader who accepts the myth of leadership will never do.

It makes it almost impossible for people in organizations to focus on results such as increasing profitability and decreasing costs because results are only valued insofar as they sustain a person's position against other individuals in the company. This leads to withholding information and resources from others, as well as trying to control others, even while blaming them for any failures. Workers who don't treat others the way they should can justify their behavior by buying into the myth. It also makes it nearly impossible to organize true teams when the implicit assumptions are that only the very few are "management material." It makes it seem as if an employee's character were fixed in a way that somehow predetermines his or her level in the organization, with only the "cream" rising to management position.

Manipulation vs. Cooperation

The sixth rank-based assumption concerns how to manage employees.

Rank-Based Assumption
You must manage (manipulate) employees to get them to do what you want.

Peer-Based Assumption
You don't manage peers; you cooperate with them.

I was once asked by a regional vice president to deliver some out-of-the-box leadership training to a group of salespeople. They all worked for the company that created the training I was to deliver. In fact, they sold the training to companies on the East Coast. I was told that most of these sales leaders had not had the opportunity to see the content of the training, so the objective was for them to have a "live" workshop experience. So that's what I prepared. Unfortunately, it was only after I began the training, and they all started vigorously protesting, that I realized we had been set up.

It seems that the regional VP perceived this group of sales representatives as troublemakers who asked too many questions. The VP figured that by attending a leadership seminar together, they'd learn to be more compliant to his wishes, but he knew they'd never agree to come to such an event. So, he told them it would be sales training, while hiding this important point from me. When they saw they were not in sales training, that they had been misled, I became the scapegoat for the absent VP who was two thousand miles away. The VP, in classic rank-based fashion, knew he could not win support for himself or his ideas through discussions, so he would have to resort to manipulation and some trickery instead. I felt sorry for this man. Though he felt superior to these sales reps by virtue of his position, he was also afraid of them and afraid to speak to them as peers, out of concern that his own lack of competence would be revealed—bursting the illusion of his leadership.

UNDESIRABLE RESULTS OF
THE MYTH OF LEADERSHIP

So far I have identified the following undesirable consequences of the myth of leadership:

- Perception that success (or failure) is due to the people at the top, thereby undervaluing the majority of the employees
- Huge inequity in pay
- Belief that the few are meant to lead and the rest to follow, fostering the creation of a culture of secrecy and deceit
- Growing gap between decision makers and reality due to that culture
- Underutilization of skills in the organization
- Fewer innovative strategies
- Less competitiveness at both strategic and tactical (operational efficiencies) levels
- Fewer humane and dignified workplaces

THE INFLUENCE OF ASSUMPTIONS

By rejecting the myth of leadership, we can create peer-based organizations where everyone does their best to help the company achieve results, and where true teams—not just teamwork—can be organized. Dismissing the myth is easier said than done, however, as we're all affected by its assumptions. For proof, read the following description and then write down a few thoughts that describe what kind of person this is.

> Works in a factory, reads a newspaper, goes to the movies, is of average height, cracks jokes, is strong and active.

Now ask an associate to read the following description and do the same, without letting the associate read either the first description or your response.

> Works in a factory, reads a newspaper, goes to the movies,
> is of average height, is intelligent, cracks jokes,
> is strong and active.

This experiment was carried out by Haire and Grunes (1950), and their findings reveal the presence of the beliefs of the myth of leadership. If you compare your description with your associates', you might find the same results as they did. The addition of the word *intelligent* in the second description elicits a different response. Most people will characterize this person as a foreman or manager in the factory, unlike the person in the first description, even though it is exactly the same as the first except for the addition of that word *intelligent*. We have all internalized the myth to such an extent that it severely clouds our common sense and judgment, and we willingly give up our freedom to those above us in rank. Looking at table 2, we can see how the contrast in rank- versus peer-based assumptions leads to very different perceptions of people and relationships in organizations.

The command-and-control style of management perpetuated by rank-based thinking has made organizational life "solitary, poor, nasty, brutish, and short" for leaders and workers alike. This should not be. Life in organizations should be communal, rich, rewarding, fulfilling, and joyful. This can only happen if we reject the myth of leadership and properly understand how to manage in a way that is harmonious with peer-based thinking.

CONCLUSION

The myth of leadership includes beliefs about motivation, human nature, and the romantic notion of a few heroic, gifted individuals. These beliefs—born of Newtonian science, the Enlightenment, and Romanticism—provide the dominant and unquestioned context for business organizations in which the few lead and the many follow.

TABLE 2: RANK- VS. PEER-BASED ASSUMPTIONS

Rank-Based Assumptions	Peer-Based Assumptions
Employees are by nature lazy and need external motivation.	Employees tend to be productive and self-motivated.
Employees are by nature selfish and self-seeking and therefore need external control to keep them in line.	Employees tend to be caring and willing to cooperate.
Leaders are heroic individuals who have risen above the masses—possessing either an innate or learned genius. They are better than those beneath them, thus have the right to control decision making in organizations and do all the commanding and controlling.	Leaders are no different than employees—they have their own unique strengths and weaknesses.
The heroic leader can control a complex organization from the top down, can accurately predict what is going to happen in the future, and should therefore be making all the critical decisions.	Only with input and participation from all levels of the organization can leaders make effective decisions about current and future business conditions.
Employees tend not to know the best thing to do, while leaders do know.	Individuals closest to where the work is done have a good grasp on what needs to happen.
You must manage (manipulate) employees to get them to do what you want.	You don't manage peers; you cooperate with them.

These beliefs provide the justification for rank-based forms of organization that do not serve human dignity, meaning, and joy. Our concept of leadership, no matter how benign, is a rank-based concept and adopts almost of necessity the assumptions of the myth of leadership. Now is the time to ask the explicit question, Why have leaders? We explore that question in detail in chapter 3.

CHAPTER 3

WHY HAVE LEADERS?

To be a lone chief atop a pyramid is abnormal and corrupting.
None of us are perfect by ourselves, and all of us need the help
and correcting influence of close colleagues. When someone is
moved atop a pyramid, that person no longer has colleagues,
only subordinates. Even the frankest and bravest of subordinates
do not talk with their boss in the same way that they talk with
their colleagues who are equals, and normal communication pat-
terns become warped. **—Robert Greenleaf,** *Servant Leadership*

I was thinking of Greenleaf's (1977) analysis of the chief–subordinate
relationship as I watched the media coverage of the recent corporate
scandals. As I listened to the accounts of the lives and times of these
disgraced corporate leaders, Greenleaf's words seemed perfectly appli-
cable. The corruption of communication caused by rank-based relationships damages everyone involved—even the leaders suffer. The
inevitable consequences of this "image of omniscience" of rank-based
leaders are a very real loneliness, indecisiveness, and recently, civil and
criminal charges!

These are not evil or bad men. They seem, in fact, quite surprised that people even see them in those terms. It is obvious that they are bewildered that their judgments and decisions are even challenged. After all, they were only doing what the myth of leadership expects of leaders of large, important, hierarchical corporations. In some sense, they are as much victims of the myth as the thousands of other people hurt by their actions and decisions, even if they did protect themselves financially from the debacle. They, too, were deceived. What deceived them, and what they used as well to deceive others, was their understanding of leadership.

To this point, I have contrasted two types of thinking in organizations: rank-based thinking and peer-based thinking—and how the former is supported by a set of assumptions that constitute what I call the myth of leadership. This myth creates organizations where the very few control all the decision-making power and leave the vast majority with little meaningful influence and authority. As a result, these organizations use very little of their creativity or innovative power. Rank-based organizations are much less productive than they could be, as the hearts and minds of most employees remain unengaged. This raises an interesting question. If our understanding of leadership is tied up with rank-based thinking, which creates unhealthy and less effective organizations, *why have leaders at all?* To answer this question, we'll need to examine the logic that makes "leaders" necessary.

LEADERSHIP MENTALITY

Over the past two decades, the field of management has been swamped with books with "leadership" in the title. Leadership training, leadership seminars, leadership gurus are everywhere in organizations and throughout the business culture. I was part of this growth industry as a presenter for one of the largest leadership training companies in the world. As I traveled extensively giving leadership seminars, I slowly began to realize the limited value derived from the huge sums of money companies spent on creating leaders. What I observed was that results, if any, seldom lasted beyond the short term. Individual lives were sometimes touched, but organizational dynamics remained unaffected. Good managers stayed good managers, and poor managers stayed poor managers—there were few if any transformations. What could be counted on to change was an increase in the cynicism of rank-and-file employees, who viewed the training as a distraction at best and managerial manipulation at worst. But the fundamental rank-based thinking remained unchallenged.

Physicist and social thinker David Bohm in his *On Dialogue* (1996) said, "Now, the whole of society has been organized to believe that we can't function without leaders. But maybe we can" (15). His statement struck me like a bolt of lightning and made me reflect on the nature of leadership and its role in organizations. It reminded me of the critique of the nature of power by French philosopher Michel Foucault. He examined the way we passively allow ourselves to be classified by the various power structures in society.[2] We acquiesce and allow these rank-based structures to categorize us and define our identity—and then determine, if we want to be a leader, what we had better be like and what habits we ought to possess.

In this climate, we become so "neurologically hardwired" to see relationships as being rank based that it becomes very difficult for us to believe it could be any other way. Most people would have a difficult time even imagining an organization, or a world, without rank-based leaders.

---

2. Michel Foucault said there are three ways of becoming classified or defined in modern society; the first he called "dividing practices," where some social or political authority classifies individuals and places them somewhere in a political hierarchy. The second he called "scientific classification," where a science authority classifies people in terms of scientific categories. Both of these methods are passive and inauthentic. The third method he termed "self-subjectification," where an individual actively defines him- or herself and is a meaning-giving self. See Foucault, *Power/Knowledge: Selected Interviews and Other Writings, 1972–1977*, ed. Colin Gordon (London: Harvester, 1980).

FUNDAMENTAL ATTRIBUTION ERROR

The main difficulty in imagining a world without rank-based leaders might be expressed in something called fundamental attribution error, or FAE—attributing a false cause to an effect.[3] For instance, in the "Great Man" (or "Terrible Man") theory of history, events occur as they do because of the temperament or character of the individuals involved. An example of this is the simplistic belief that people do good things because they're good and bad things because they're bad. This is, observation has taught me, a fundamental attribution error.

Character is a bundle of habits and potential behaviors that depend on timing, circumstances, or context to be triggered. Research has shown that context can make good people do terrible things and terrible people do extraordinarily good things. How we behave is frequently a function of context rather than character. This is demonstrated by research by Stanley Milgram of Yale University in the 1960s showing that average, decent people would give an electric shock to a stranger for giving wrong answers in the context of a faked scientific experiment.[4]

Another example is the 1973 study by Princeton psychologists John Darley and Daniel Batson. As described by Malcolm Gladwell in *The Tipping Point* (2000), Darley and Batson based their study on the Biblical story of the Good Samaritan. They chose to work with a group of seminarians, people who had chosen a career of helping others. They gave each seminarian the assignment to prepare a short talk on a given Biblical theme, and he or she was to walk over to a nearby building to deliver the talk. Some were even given as a topic the story

3. Malcolm Gladwell discusses FAE in *The Tipping Point: How Little Things Can Make a Big Difference* (New York: Little Brown & Co., 2000), 160.

4. See Milgram's own analysis of this basic human phenomenon in *Obedience to Authority: An Experimental View* (New York: HarperCollins, 1983).

of the Good Samaritan. On the way, each student would run into a person slumped in an alley with his head down, coughing and groaning. The intent was to see who would stop and help. Of the variables in this study, the only one that seemed to matter was that some students were told they were late and needed to hurry and others were told they had a few minutes and could walk over more leisurely. Of those told they were late, only 10 percent stopped to help. Of those told they had more time, 65 percent stopped. The logical implication of this study is clear: a person's character or "conviction of heart" is far less important to actual behavior than the context for that behavior. This works in the other direction as well—bad people do good things, too.

If context, not character, is the determining factor, then a key question is, How do we organize things and create the organizational environment for exercising our better habits? Does rank-based leadership create the right context for a full flowering of human potential?

Rank in History

We tend to think that leaders are necessary for effectively guiding human relationships in organizations, but do we ever ask why we believe this? Why do we anoint a relatively small number of individuals as leaders and give them more resources and better assignments, while we lock the vast majority into positions that offer little hope of fully engaging their potential talents? If we look at the history of human social organizations, we see that we have been attracted to command-and-control, rank-based forms of social organization. Following Joseph Tainter's analysis of these organization types in *The Collapse of Complex Societies* (1988), we can identify three basic types of human organization. The first two are categorized as "simple"; the third as "complex." All three of these social forms have been established on rank-based relationships:

- **"Big Man" society**—right to rule determined by virtue of personality; control maintained through threat of physical force; individual's status determined by proximity to the Big Man

- **Chieftain society**—right to rule determined by position rather than personality; control maintained through threat of physical force, not from individuals, but from the organization; individual's status determined by position

- **Hierarchical society**—occurring over the last six thousand years; multilevel rank-based structure with the highest level controlling power; control maintained through threat of loss of position

In each of these forms, a person's standing and position in society are based on rank. Status and access to resources depend on proximity to the Big Man, the tribal chief, or the person at the top of the hierarchy. To keep relative standing and position safe, individuals must keep the rank-based leaders above them happy. It seems that rank-based organizations, in some sense, have been set as our default position since the days of the Big Man, when societies typically numbered no more than one thousand. This historical context has produced a rank-based logic that requires a division of leaders and followers. It is sufficient to say that rank-based organizations represent our past but not the promise of our future. A fourth social form, the network society, is emerging.

NETWORK SOCIETY

Today we are transitioning from a hierarchical society to a network society that favors peer-based relationships. The network society does not automatically privilege rank, so in cases where genuine communication will occur only between peers, networks ensure that the individual is not trapped in a limited perspective that does not accurately reflect reality. Because flow is more important than power, individuals who facilitate processes will be more valued than positions in static hierarchies. Networks reflect the assumptions of peer-based thinking and conflict with the assumptions of rank-based thinking, especially when it comes to addressing power and other people.

Peer-based organizations will have a competitive advantage over rank-based companies in the network society. With help from the work of Manuel Castells in *The Rise of the Network Society* (1996) we can identify some of the characteristics of this kind of society:

- No single centralized authority, but multiple centers of decision making that are globally interdependent

- Different, yet parallel, paths of systems and processes making the network society resilient yet incredibly open and adaptable to a changing environment

- Ability to expand without limits and to innovate without threatening its balance

- Open communication and information flowing across all domains of human activity and experience

- Belief that process is more important and powerful than position, and that the key resource is neither land nor capital, but knowledge and information

Networks apply the logic of peer-based management for decision making and for the meaning of individual identity and human relationships in organizations—fundamentally different from the management logic in rank-based organizations. It's commonly said that you lead people and manage things, but I suggest that leading, as we understand it today, is a rank-based practice that will no longer serve our social and organizational contexts. In peer-based organizations, the practice of management will exclude leaders as we have come to understand the concept. It's not about learning a new gimmick or technique to "lead," something that all employees know is just another attempt to manipulate them to get more for less. It's about rejecting rank-based thinking altogether and the false belief that a single person, or just a few persons, at the top of the organization create its success or failure. Again, networks require a different logic from that of hierarchies to be successful—a peer-based logic as opposed to rank-based logic.

RANK-BASED LOGIC
VS. PEER-BASED LOGIC

Logic is the explicit or implicit set of norms or rules with which we judge and make decisions in organizations. Depending on whether you make rank- or peer-based assumptions, you will use specific criteria in making critical decisions. Frequently these criteria are left unspoken or not even fully recognized by the decision maker, but the logic of our false assumptions in rank-based organizations creates decision making that does not serve human dignity and growth. Characteristics of each type of logic are outlined in table 3 and discussed in detail below.

Exclusive vs. Inclusive

Rank-based logic regards leadership as an opportunity to be offered only to a few.

Rank-Based Logic
Power positions are reserved for the select few who climb to the top of the organization.

TABLE 3: RANK- VS. PEER-BASED LOGIC	
Rank-Based Logic	**Peer-Based Logic**
Exclusive	Inclusive
Commanding	Influencing
Domineering	Participating
Scarcity based	Abundance based
Individualistic	Community formulated
Inequitable	Equitable

Peer-Based Logic

Everyone is invited to be a mentor to others and a creator of value, to participate in decision making, and to share in the exercise of power.

Rank-based logic creates an exclusive club. Your identity and value arbitrarily follow from your position in the hierarchy, and you genuinely relate only to those of the same rank. To support this club, organizations select individuals, put them through "cookie cutter" leadership development programs, and hope they come out the other end as leaders. Now they should have all the right habits and characteristics to act the part and fit into the hierarchy and the position that awaits them. In the process, however, these individuals become suspicious of their own unique and wonderful qualities that would allow them to make great and original contributions. Perhaps even more insidiously, such programs tend to reinforce an already common belief that our organizations should be rank based, where a fortunate few are placed in superior positions over the less fortunate many.

Peer-based logic creates an inclusive, participatory organization. There is no sense of a "top" of the organization and no exclusive club to belong to or protect. In the absence of rank, all members of the organization are peers, so genuine communication flourishes and productivity is high. It is a logic where a diversity of talents and abilities can be recognized within the realm of equality of worth and value. It brings in many different viewpoints and interpretations to better understand the world. Peer-based logic makes organizations wiser.

Commanding vs. Influencing

"Command and control" is the key phrase in rank-based logic.

Rank-Based Logic
Power is defined as command and control over things and people.

Peer-Based Logic
Power is defined as influence on things and people.

Rank-based logic seeks to coerce cooperation. Yet commanding a subordinate produces only compliance and dependence. Again, because of rank, the meaning and value of your life are falsely determined by how many people are above you and therefore can command and control you, versus how many people are below you, meaning you can command and control them. Such deliberate top-down management structures are very time consuming. When business conditions are changing constantly, it's essential to respond quickly—something that autocratic, secretive, hierarchical organizations do very poorly. Rank-based logic tends to be inflexible and cannot respond quickly to rapid changes in the business environment. Commanding, also, as a rank-based concept, tends to develop the talents of only a select few while underutilizing the talents of the majority.

MOTEK

One company that puts peer-based logic into practice is Motek, a twelve-year-old software company based in Beverly Hills, California. At Motek, all employees participate in organizational decisions, from office furnishings to job assignments to bonuses. There is no fear of failure, because there is no one higher up from whom to fear reprisal, so innovative solutions to problems are more likely. In a personal e-mail communication, founder Ann Price told me, "At Motek we believe in rewarding communication even if it's communication about failure." Their motto is "Fail sooner; succeed more often." Motek's inclusive approach to managing work engages the whole person. Price continued, "At Motek we believe that it's impossible to manage people. We can only manage process." In a peer-based organization, people manage themselves and cooperate with others in managing processes.

Peer-based logic posits that influencing others creates commitment—practicing the power of subtle influence evokes cooperation within the organization. Respect and commitment from others, as determined by the integrity of your choices, are what genuinely give meaning and value to your life. At W. L. Gore & Associates, the maker of Gore-Tex waterproof fabric (profiled in greater detail in chapter 4), there are no designated leaders. No one can command anyone else to do anything. If an employee needs assistance on some project, the employee must persuade other associates to join in the work. Such peer-based logic has created a remarkable spirit of cooperation at Gore, a company that even in times of economic recession has remained profitable.

Domineering vs. Participating

"Dominate and you will win" is the attitude of leaders who use rank-based logic.

Rank-Based Logic
You must dominate, intimidate, and use fear to motivate employees.

Peer-Based Logic
Getting things done is the natural path for people; people are self-motivated.

An extremely bright and dedicated executive called me one day. He was the vice president overseeing the software engineers in his organization. He told me that his engineers were unmotivated and not committed to the company. He wanted to give them an ultimatum: Either pledge commitment to the company or leave! I persuaded him to meet with me first. Over lunch, he filled me in on what was happening. I could tell he desired the best for the company as well as for the engineers. He truly wanted them to excel. Yet his thinking was dominated by rank-based logic. He planned to invite the underperforming team of engineers to a hotel room, where he would tell them what he thought their problem was and what he thought they should do. He was then going to have them stand against one of the walls in the room and ask them one at a time if they would commit to his vision. They would demonstrate their commitment by walking across the room to the other wall. Those who walked would still have a job; those who didn't would be fired.

In all sincerity, he believed this was what a leader should do—make the hard decisions and demand loyalty. He could imagine no other way. Fortunately, he was also a reasonable man who would listen to counsel. I laid out for him why his plan would only antagonize the engineers and make the problem worse. Even those who walked across the room would check out of the organization with their hearts and minds. He would have their bodies, but not their passion. People support best what they themselves create.

We discussed an alternative strategy where I would facilitate a peer-based team analysis of their situation and possible solutions. He agreed to the meeting and to approach it not as the leader who would tell them what to do, but as an associate who was asking for their participation in solving a common problem. I enjoyed two fabulous days with him and his team of engineers, and we made real progress in creating a dynamic and successful peer-based team.

Peer-based logic tells us that if things are not getting done, or people are not motivated, it is because something is blocking them. It asserts that all problems and blocks are visible and that solutions are obvious to at least a few people in the organization. So, it invites participation in problem solving. At Motek, no one is told what to do or how to do it. Each employee is assumed to be competent and motivated to do excellent work. At the start of each week, Motek's software engineers gather to review needed tasks and projects. As they go down the list, each will volunteer to accomplish one or more of the assignments. No one is supposed to take on more work than he or she can accomplish in a week. On Thursday they meet to communicate to each other which of their assignments they would be able to complete by Friday. They then can arrange to help each other out if needed.

Scarcity Based vs. Abundance Based

With rank-based logic, everything is in scarce supply, including what people are willing to give.

Rank-Based Logic
People are selfish and unwilling to share.

Peer-Based Logic
People are willing to cooperate and share with those who cooperate and share with them.

Rank-based logic characterizes people as basically selfish and unwilling to share their resources, knowledge, or time. So you must ruthlessly compete to get your fair share before somebody else takes it from you. Of course, time and resources can be in short supply in the company, but knowledge is a resource that has no external constraints. In an information- and network-based society, knowledge shared with others can be used to find ways to create more time and resources. But, with the rank-based logic of scarcity, knowledge is withheld and all other assets decrease proportionately.

Peer-based logic characterizes people as altruistic and eager to share resources, knowledge, and time to create more success for all. We see that there is enough for everyone, and more can be created through shared effort. We leverage the knowledge-based talents of everyone in the organization to find ways to expand the pie and create abundance. Through peer-based logic we realize that the more a company shares the organizational wealth with all members, the more commitment and dedication it will receive.

Motek, for example, gives every employee, after ten years with the company, a leased Lexus LS300, or an automobile of similar value. Each employee has five weeks of vacation, and no one is allowed to work past 5 P.M. or on weekends. Because Motek believes employees should avoid long, stressful commutes, Motek subsidizes their purchase of residences in the Beverly Hills neighborhood.

Individualistic vs. Community Formulated

There is no sense of community in rank-based logic.

Rank-Based Logic

People at work are just replaceable cogs in the machinery of business.

Peer-Based Logic

People are by nature social animals who seek and enjoy working with others.

With rank-based logic, people see work as a burden and organizations as a necessary evil. We only grudgingly join up with organizations and then find life within them to be nasty, boring, and deadening to the spirit. When the organization encounters hardships, the assumption is that those below should be sacrificed to protect the privilege of those above. All too frequently we read in the financial section of the paper about this type of logic in action: another CEO who laid off hundreds of workers is awarded with a fat bonus at the end of the year.

Author Jason Jennings, in a *USA Today* (2002) editorial, said that many leaders believe downsizing in tough economic times is the right leadership thing to do. Citing a major 2002 research project of The Business Roundtable on the relationship between layoffs and productivity, Jennings challenges this conventional wisdom. The research revealed that the world's most productive firms make an explicit promise never to balance the books through layoffs. Instead, they look for more creative ways to cut costs and increase demand.

After evaluating the finances of more than 4,000 public and private firms worldwide, my research team and I settled on 80 that topped their peers by every reasonable measure of productivity. Simply put, these firms sold more, spent less and made more profit per employee than their competition, year after year.

The most striking trait these 80 productivity superstars shared was their passionate opposition to layoffs, even when the economy was in the dumps. Consider Nucor, America's largest steel maker, which manufactures rolled steel and steel joists. Nucor has reduced the time it takes to produce a ton of steel from 11 hours to 30 minutes—while increasing its earnings for 30 years in a row.

In line with this study, peer-based logic stems from the fact that people are by nature social animals who seek and enjoy life with others in equitable work institutions. Because of the community orientation, everyone shares in both the sacrifices and the good times—perhaps a greater portion is shared by those who can afford it. As Ann Price told me about Motek, "We believe that everything depends on the health of the group." This peer-based logic makes good economic sense.

Inequitable vs. Equitable

Rank-based logic produces a serious imbalance in the way rewards are distributed.

Rank-Based Logic

Those higher in rank are entitled to a far greater share of the organization's resources in the form of compensation than those lower in rank.

Peer-Based Logic

Distributing the organization's resources more equitably in the organization will generate far greater returns to everyone in the long run.

Rank-based logic asserts that the large and growing gap between the salaries of the top executives and those of the frontline workers is natural and justified given the disparity in contributions leaders make compared to everyone else. It asserts that there is nothing anyone can do about the gross disparity in pay and compensation between the top and bottom of the organization—that's just the way the game is played, so everyone should take advantage of it when they get to the top.

Peer-based logic retorts that this attitude is a result of the myth of leadership and does not reflect reality—that the growing gap in salaries is a serious threat to the long-term viability of organizations and the communities they build. Gross inequities in pay make true community unachievable and genuine relationships impossible. Those organizations that achieve a real sense of solidarity have checks on excessive executive pay and more team-based compensation. At Motek, for example, there are only three pay levels, with no level more than $30,000 above or below the adjacent level. Management also realized that compensation practices and monetary rewards have to be tied to collective performance, not individual performance.

Epidemiologist Richard Wilkinson has spent a lot of time studying the effects of income inequality in social organizations. In *Unhealthy Societies: The Afflictions of Inequality* (1996), he points out that "among the developed countries it is not the richest societies that have the best health, but those that have the smallest income differences" (28). In his work, Wilkinson has shown both how income disparities create unhealthy organizations and how rank distinctions create a culture of dominance that diminishes the welfare of all. Although his work is focused on social organizations, I believe his findings are easily reflected in business organizations as well. The lesson is both clear and unmistakable: rank-based logic and inequities create unhealthy organizations.

CONCLUSION

Why have leaders? The answer is, because rank-based logic requires it. Our whole concept of supervisors and managers follows the logic of rank-based, not peer-based, companies. The concept of individuals as either leaders or followers springs from a rank-based society, not a peer-based one. When we see one another as peers, there are no leaders and there are no followers. One day linking, not ranking, will be the primary power relationship in our social experience. Peer-based management will be not just the superior way morally, but competitively as well. Peer-based organizations will no longer have professional or tenured leaders.

A change of our social experience toward networks and away from rank and hierarchy alone will not eliminate the unhealthy context in which we understand our identity and the meaning of our relationships in terms of leaders and followers. The new social context of networks, however, will give competitive advantage to peer-based organizations and create better business opportunities to those who construct their sense of self and relationships to others within peer-based thinking. So-called leaderless organizations will gain momentum. Before looking at leaderless organizations, however, we need to examine the final aspect of rank- versus peer-based thinking, namely organizational practices.

PART TWO

THE EVOLUTION OF ORGANIZATIONAL PRACTICES

CHAPTER 4

"STRANGE ATTRACTORS" AND ORGANIZATIONAL PRACTICES

Ever since my imagination was captured by the phrase "strange attractor," I have wondered if we could identify such a force in organizations. Is there a magnetic force, a basin for activity, so attractive that it pulls all behavior toward it and creates coherence? My current belief is that we do have such attractors at work in organizations and that one of the most potent shapers of behavior in organizations, and in life, is meaning.

—Margaret Wheatley, *Leadership and the New Science*

When I think about business and organizations through the perspective of other disciplines, such as art and science, I become more creative in solving organizational problems. Chaos theory, for example, has given me some significant insights into business and rank-based versus peer-based practices.

Up to this point, we've compared and contrasted rank-based and peer-based assumptions and logic. We've seen how the myth of leadership creates unhealthy and unproductive organizations. In this chapter we look at how rank-based thinking, as the foundation of the myth of leadership, leads to a set of organizational practices that not only fail to fully engage employees but also leave the majority of their creativity and energy untapped. In contrast is peer-based thinking and the peer-based practices employed by some very successful organizations. We begin, however, with an investigation into chaos theory.

CHAOS THEORY

Science affects the way we think together. Like music and other forms of artistic expression, science gives an educated person new eyes with which to view the world. I remember one time when we were living in Cambridge, Massachusetts, my son, Ryan, who was in the first grade, came home from school and with great excitement told me that if a butterfly flapped its wings in China, it could change the weather in Cambridge. What he was referring to is an ancient Chinese proverb that says that the power of a butterfly's wings can be felt on the other side of the world. The proverb implies the effect of natural processes, that small changes in the input can produce huge changes in the output. This is the origin of the now famous "butterfly effect" described in chaotic systems, one of the well-known popularizations of chaos theory.

Like the butterfly, a business organization, by tapping into the heart and mind of each employee, can unleash infinite possibilities—small changes in the input can produce huge changes in the output. Organizations can be endlessly creative and innovative, or they can be unimaginative and uninspired. It depends on the key practices each organization chooses to reward and toward which "attractors" of meaning they will be drawn.

QUALITIES OF SYSTEMS AND "STRANGE ATTRACTORS"

Chaos theory explains how complex systems evolve. Quite surprisingly, while the number of complex systems might be nearly endless, in their evolution they will be attracted to only four predictable and ordered states, called attractors. The word *attractor* was chosen because the long-term behavior of the system's many parts seems pulled toward one of four different, predictable states, producing a predictable shape to the eventual system. In the course of a system's evolution, how that system settles into one and not another of the attractors is determined by three qualities:

- Energy flow into the system
- Degrees of freedom in the system
- Flexibility in the structure of the system

The higher the energy flow, the greater the degrees of freedom, and the more flexible the structure will allow the system to evolve toward the great creativity and endless possibilities of the "strange attractor," the most commonly known of the four attractors.[5]

THE STRANGE ATTRACTOR AND RESILIENCY OF PEER ORGANIZATIONS

We've seen that systems evolve from simple and uninteresting to complex, dynamic, and endlessly creative as the system's energy flow, degrees of freedom, and flexibility are all increased. Organizations

5. For more information on attractors, see John Briggs and F. David Peat, *Turbulent Mirror* (New York: Harper & Row, 1989).

likewise become more innovative and successful by implementing the peer-based practices that increase information flow, freedom in decision making, and the flexibility and responsiveness of the organization.

A strange attractor, simply put, is a system that appears chaotic but in fact possesses an amazing degree of order and creative potential. A key property of the strange attractor is its "stretch and fold" characteristic. Imagine taking some bread dough and placing two raisins in it side by side. If you stretch the dough, the two raisins move far apart, but when you fold the dough back in on itself, the two raisins once again are side by side. If you repeat this procedure again and again, you will notice how the two raisins wander randomly in the dough, with one stretch moving them away from each other and one fold moving them closer together, all the while not altering the general shape of the dough. If you think of the dough as the attractor of the system and the positions of the raisins as two different states of the system, you get a good picture of what happens in a chaotic system. At any one moment in the history of a dynamic system, two events or states are in close proximity, while in the very next moment they are unpredictably far apart. This is due to the nearly infinite degrees of freedom available in the strange attractor system.

Another way to explain this property of the strange attractor is to view the system as being formed by two antagonistic tendencies: (1) a tendency to converge, to fold, and (2) a tendency to diverge, to stretch. This makes the system incredibly resilient. Similarly, an organization in today's turbulent business environment, with its high rates of energy circulation, must be able to deal with both tension-expanding (stretch) and tension-compressing (fold) forces. Organizations need to be able to *stretch* to accommodate special needs and then to return to shape, or *fold* back. They must be able to deal with uncertainty by flexibly changing structure when necessary and then reconfiguring without breaking apart. The peer-based practices that we will discuss give an organization this responsiveness and flexibility. Rank-based thinking is inadequate in this "strange" world. It will break apart under the stress of uncertainty and turbulence. Companies need to develop the elasticity and the plasticity that is characteristic of the stretching and folding of the strange attractor. The implications of the strange attractor model for organizations, especially leaderless organizations, will be seen later in this chapter and in subsequent chapters.

RANK-BASED VS. PEER-BASED PRACTICES

As in chaos theory, where an increase in the energy, freedom, and flexibility of the system brings great creativity and variety, in organizational theory, if you increase the information flow, freedom in decision making, and flexibility in relationships, you'll open the company up to greater creativity and innovation. This requires peer-based practices rather than rank-based practices, which can cause companies to squander so much of the competencies and skills of their people. To better understand how to unleash the great potential of all employees to capture the magic of the strange attractor, we now need to compare and contrast two different types of practices as outlined in table 4 and discussed in detail.

TABLE 4: RANK- VS. PEER-BASED PRACTICES	
Rank-Based Practices	**Peer-Based Practices**
Controlling	Sharing
Mindless	Mindful
Top down	Freeing
Fearful	Creative
Bureaucratic	Flexible
Communicating deceptively	Communicating honestly

Controlling vs. Sharing

Controlling is not only a way of thinking, but also a practice influenced by rank-based logic.

Rank-Based Practice
Maintain tight control and protection of information from those outside management; secrecy is important; share information only on a need-to-know basis, if at all.

Peer-Based Practice
Promote open flow and sharing of information, including knowledge of business and financial conditions—with no secrets and no surprises.

I have consulted with many companies where the senior executives hold on tight to information that would be in the best interest of the organization for everyone to know. In the absence of the free flow of information in rank-based organizations, the climate is often rife with damaging rumors. Information is, of course, power, and when it is held by the few, it creates high levels of distrust. In difficult times this rank-based practice destroys productivity in companies as the majority of employees engage in endless gossiping and cautious, self-protective behavior. That outcome contrasts sharply with what happens in an organization that employs peer-based practices. One of the best examples of this type of organization is SRC Holdings (see p. 65).

Mindless vs. Mindful

Another rank-based practice affects the stretching of the mind.

Rank-Based Practice
Demand that employees do as they're told.

SRC HOLDINGS

SRC Holdings Corporation of Springfield, Missouri, became well-known through its president and CEO, Jack Stack. In his book with Bo Burlingame, *The Great Game of Business* (2002), Mr. Stack recounts how he and some partners instituted an organizational system to create a culture of ownership that came to be called "open-book management." In their culture they have a strict policy against secrets, and they open up all the company's financial statements to employees. Stack says of this business practice, "When you open your books—really open them—you also open your mind, and neither your mind nor your books will be closed again. Why? Because you'll keep discovering things about yourself and your company you wouldn't have known otherwise" (9).

Following this peer-based practice, their company has consistently grown 15 percent a year. They have seen their stock price climb from a low of 10 cents to over $80 per share. Each SRC employee thinks and acts like an owner and is constantly searching for ways to increase productivity and lower costs. Like the strange attractor that is endlessly creative, organizations that open the flow of information with this peer-based practice become endlessly innovative!

Peer-Based Practice
Encourage employees to think strategically.

When secrets are kept and information is scarce, most employees adopt self-protective behaviors. They don't act until told to do so and then drag their feet, complain about resources or lack of training, and grumble that what they have to do is pointless anyway. These are natural survival instincts that dominate in a rank-based organization. Rank-based managers find they have to resort to bribes and threats to get employees to do things. They gripe that employees lack initiative, but fail to see that they do not provide adequate information and are all too ready to cut off the neck of anyone who sticks it out too far. The outcome of managing work this way, where both the manager and the managed believe it's safer to just do what they're told, is gridlock and a stagnant business.

Peers, on the other hand, lead themselves and cooperate with others. You don't manage your peers, you collaborate with them. Jack Stack realized that by increasing the flow of information through the organization, all employees would begin to act like an owner and to *think strategically*. So instead of waiting until told what to do, employees begin to take responsibility for making things happen. They bring within themselves the passion, vision, and motivation to do the job.

Top Down vs. Freeing

Comparing rank-based and peer-based practices reveals an obvious fork in the road of decision making.

Rank-Based Practice
Employ top-down, command-and-control management and decision making, where the few are treated and rewarded as leaders and the many are treated and rewarded as followers.

Peer-Based Practice
Give all members of the organization the authority to make the decisions affecting their work—expanding freedom and creating soft hierarchies.

W. L. GORE & ASSOCIATES

A peer-based organization knows that increasing degrees of freedom in the company and allowing greater participation in decision making will result in a more creative and energized work environment. One such company is W. L. Gore & Associates, Inc., based in Newark, Delaware. Since 1959, Gore has thrived within a work environment lacking a fixed hierarchy or formal leadership titles. Bill Gore, the founder, envisioned an organization with the following characteristics:

- No fixed or assigned authority

- Natural leadership defined by natural followership

- Objectives established by consensus

- Person-to-person communication encouraged

- Tasks and functions organized by commitments

Gore has been consistently profitable and innovative by increasing the freedom of communication and decision making for all employees. Any Gore associate (in the absence of formal titles, all employees are called associates) with a good idea is free to communicate it to anyone else in the company. If the associate can persuade enough people that the idea would be profitable—and can attract a cross-functional team to design, manufacture, market, and sell the idea—then it happens. By the way, in 2002 sales at Gore topped $1.4 billion.

A big mistake many organizations make with their people is thinking that only those individuals who desire leadership positions desire to participate in decision making, thereby ignoring those individuals who could be making wonderful contributions to the organization's decision making. The myth of leadership falsely leads us to think that decision making is the sole prerogative of leaders, and those who do not seek leadership positions are weak or lazy. This belief leads to a rank-based organizational practice of very little freedom and thus very little creativity.

Fearful vs. Creative

Fear of making mistakes reduces creativity in rank-based practices.

Rank-Based Practice
Warn employees not to make mistakes.

Peer-Based Practice
Encourage employees to be creative and learn constantly.

Rank-based organizations restrict freedom and hope that by doing so they can reduce mistakes. "Don't make mistakes!" is a key directive at such an organization, but instead of eliminating mistakes, it eliminates innovation. Another point that rank-based companies frequently overlook is that success misleads, whereas failure educates. Without the freedom to fail, employees and the organization will, paradoxically, keep making the same mistakes over and over again. I recall hearing about a very empowering manager. He brought all new hires into his office and told them, "You're 'preforgiven' for all the mistakes that I hope you'll make. However," he went on, "I do expect you to tell me when you fail and also to tell me what you learned from your failure." His peer-based department at this otherwise rank-based organization always outperformed the other departments, and it was the department that employees from the rest of the organization most wanted to transfer into.

W. L. GORE & ASSOCIATES

Freedom to be creative and constantly learning is a key peer-based practice. This freedom can also be risky, but W. L. Gore has created the right habits to make it work. Associates are trained to consult with other associates on any major decision and to ask certain "waterline" questions to ensure that the decision reflects and supports the organization's strategic direction and well-being. The two questions they are taught to ask are these:

- If you do it and it works, will it improve our revenue or decrease our costs?

- If you do it and it fails, can we afford it?

Only if the answer to both questions is yes do they proceed. Such freedom unleashes incredible amounts of energy and enthusiasm within the organization to drive it to new heights of success.

Bureaucratic vs. Flexible

Rank-based practices follow the Peter Principle: Promote people to the level of their incompetence.

Rank-Based Practice
Promote individuals to leadership positions in a fixed bureaucratic hierarchy, where they stay until retirement or further promotion; who you know can be more important than what you know.

Peer-Based Practice
Rotate leadership and manage key organizational decisions by inviting participation by all members of the organization into the process.

My first independent consulting job was a disaster. I came in excited to help an Internet recruitment site improve both its strategy and employee morale. My first training event on building trust was fabulous. All the employees left feeling good about the company, and I was even feeling good about the participation of the CEO. He was known less for great competence and more for leaving half-way through the day to sit at a nearby park. He had been chosen as CEO through his close friendship with the owners. But at the training he had said all the right things to give the employees hope. At the training session, groups had agreed to plans that would immediately boost the sales of their services and lead to a promising growth in revenue. The sales force consisted of extremely talented and ambitious young people—I thought this organization had a bright future, and that I would have a nice contract for some time to come. Of course, it didn't happen this way.

The very next day, when I went into his office, he acted as though the meeting and plans of the previous day had not even existed. He refused to even acknowledge there had been that conversation. I couldn't believe it. What was worse, his entire executive team acted the same way. Employee trust evaporated, and from that day forward very little work took place. Everyone had mentally checked out. The one person in a leadership position who tried to challenge the CEO's fixed and inflexible authority was slowly frozen out of leadership meetings and any decision making. Within a year the company went bankrupt, and I was out several thousand dollars. Perhaps that was a small price to pay for the lesson of learning the cost of the rank-based practice of fixed and hierarchical bureaucracy in organizations.

Peer-based organizations such as Orpheus, the "conductorless" orchestra, reject fixed, permanent hierarchical positions and the associated inflexible leadership authority in favor of rotational leadership, where key organizational decisions are made through peer-based leadership councils. Orpheus has pioneered the unique peer-

ORPHEUS CHAMBER ORCHESTRA

Certainly there are few more stressful and precise business projects than planning for, preparing for, and performing at Carnegie Hall, and the Orpheus Chamber Orchestra does it all without a formal, rank-based leader. They have found a process that better empowers the creativity, talent, passion, and productivity of each person in the organization. Leadership roles exist, but these are assigned to peers on a project-by-project basis, and with each project, core teams or councils are chartered to supervise the key decisions that must be made and communicated. Each person in the orchestra has the opportunity to take a turn at leading the collaboration and consensus decision–making process. The benefits to the organization are enormous. Harvey Seifter (Seifter and Economy 2001), an executive director at Orpheus, had this to say about the peer practice of rotational leadership:

> As more and more businesses become information-based, using fewer employees to produce expanded results, organizations where everyone has the opportunity to lead will certainly be the most successful. Companies that can tap their employees' expertise, problem-solving skills, and self-direction enjoy a serious competitive advantage: motivated and satisfied workers who consistently hit company targets and meet unexpected challenges, even when formally appointed leaders are not available. (102)

based management practice of abolishing fixed and permanent leadership positions and instead shares and rotates leadership roles. This has given them an incredibly innovative and flexible structure.

The company-killing problems I encountered on my first consulting job—the incompetent, but well-connected CEO, the fixed and unresponsive bureaucracy, the inability for anyone lower in the hierarchy to significantly influence those higher in the hierarchy—all disappear in the peer-based practice of rotational leadership. In the future, this practice will undermine the myth of leadership and allow everyone in the organization to develop his or her potential to the fullest. It will also result in greater equality of salaries and prohibit the stupid excesses of executive pay that plague most organizations today. This will boost morale, trust, and productivity better than any leadership seminar or change initiative imposed on the organization.

Communicating Deceptively vs. Communicating Honestly

Honest communication does not exist in rank-based thinking.

Rank-Based Practice
Tell those above you what they want to hear and those below you only what they "need" to know.

Peer-Based Practice
Communicate throughout the organization honestly and truthfully.

When employees believe that lines of authority and decision-making power are fixed and inflexible, they will engage in the most common rank-based practice—they will tell those above them only what they think they want to hear and those beneath them only what they think they need to know. This leads to serious communication problems. When I consult with organizations, I like to make this point by sharing a funny story that everyone in business understands. It captures the reality that people in rank-based organizations are more consistently rewarded for telling their superiors pleasant lies than for telling the truth. This lightly adapted version of a fable dating back to the early 1960s illustrates the phenomenon of a progressive disconnection of decision makers from reality.

THE PLAN

In the beginning was the Plan.

And then came the Assumptions.

And the Assumptions were without form.

And the Plan was without substance.

And darkness was upon the face of the Workers.

And they spoke among themselves, saying,
"It is a crock of crap, and it stinks."

And the Workers went unto their Supervisors and said,
"It is a pail of dung, and we can't live with the smell."

And the Supervisors went unto their Managers, saying,
"It is a container of excrement, and it is very strong, such that
none may abide by it."

And the Managers went unto their Directors, saying,
"It is a vessel of fertilizer, and none may abide its strength."

And the Directors spoke among themselves, saying to one another,
"It contains that which aids plant growth, and it is very strong."

And the Directors went to the Vice Presidents, saying unto them,
"It promotes growth, and it is very powerful."

And the Vice Presidents went to the President, saying unto him,
"This new plan will actively promote the growth and vigor of
the company with very powerful effects."

And the President looked upon the Plan and saw that it was good.

And the Plan became Policy.

And this is how shit happens.

ORGANIZATIONAL ATTRACTORS

Organizations are dynamic systems comprising many interacting parts—most important of which are its people—interacting over time. Could it be possible that, though there are thousands if not millions of human organizations with people relating to one another in an almost infinite number of ways, they might also eventually be reducible to similar basic "attractor" states? In other words, could we identify basic organizational attractors? Further, wouldn't it be the dominant practice, either rank or peer based, that would create the specific type of organization?

It is not difficult to imagine that, in the course of their interaction, relationships between humans will acquire a recurrent pattern, which might evolve into predictable structures that grow more complex over time. Hierarchy certainly is an attractor in human relationships, found wherever people interact over long periods of time. This helps explain the prominence and durability of hierarchical organizations. Hierarchy is merely an organizational attractor.

I wondered what would be the other attractors in human organizational relationships and how could understanding these shapes be of use in the management of companies, especially since the conditions today seem ripe for a decisive transition. Altogether, I found four attractors in human organizational relationships based on inspiration from chaos theory.

1. The "Big Chief" organization

2. The hierarchical organization

3. The open organization

4. The leaderless organization

How these four types of organizations factor in the evolution of an organization from rank based to peer based is described in ensuing chapters.

CONCLUSION

When an organization rejects rank-based practices and implements instead the peer-based practices I have introduced here, then all individuals will learn to speak, write, and listen persuasively. Peer-based organizations capture the power in the strange attractor by unleashing the potential in all their employees—by increasing the flow of information through the company, by increasing the freedom of decision making, and by maximizing the flexibility and responsiveness of the organization through rotational leadership. The peer-based practices we reviewed are at the heart of peer-based thinking in organizations. Table 5 combines all the aspects of peer-based thinking, from peer-based assumptions and peer-based logic to peer-based practices.

Today, as the complexity and flow of information in world markets accelerate, we are witnessing the demand by people from every race and nation for greater freedom—for the autonomy to make the decisions that affect their lives. This is pulling organizations away from conventional management practices and has opened up the need for peer-based organizational management. If we can create the space for peer-based organizations through the implementation of the correct assumptions, logic, and practices, they will naturally emerge without force or coercion and allow meaningful organizational life to evolve.

By rejecting rank-based management thinking and understanding human organizations in terms of energy flow, degrees of freedom, and structure, new possibilities open up through peer-based practices. The wisdom of peer-based management reverses the classical leadership view that only the few are meant to lead and the rest are destined to follow. This opens up the field of contribution to many more and conditions the possibility of peer-based organizations. It should be understood, however, that hierarchy itself is an important and useful type of organization required by a certain relationship of energy and structure. It is not hierarchy, but rather hierarchy along with rank-based management, that creates poor results and poor working conditions.

TABLE 5: THE FOUNDATION OF PEER-BASED ORGANIZATIONS

Peer-Based Assumptions	Peer-Based Logic	Peer-Based Practices
Employees tend to be productive and self-motivated.	Inclusive: Everyone is invited to be a mentor to others and a creator of value, to participate in decision making, and to share in the exercise of power.	Promote open flow and sharing of information, including knowledge of business and financial conditions—with no secrets and no surprises.
Employees tend to be caring and willing to cooperate.	Influencing: Power is defined as influence on things and people.	Encourage employees to think strategically.
Leaders are no different than employees—they have their own unique strengths and weaknesses.	Participating: Getting things done is the natural path for people; people are self-motivated.	Give all members of the organization the authority to make the decisions affecting their work—expanding freedom and creating soft hierarchies.

TABLE 5: THE FOUNDATION OF PEER-BASED ORGANIZATIONS cont'd

Peer-Based Assumptions	Peer-Based Logic	Peer-Based Practices
Only with input and participation from all levels of the organization can leaders make effective decisions about current and future business conditions.	Abundance based: People are willing to cooperate and share with those who cooperate and share with them.	Encourage employees to be creative and learn constantly.
Individuals closest to where the work is done have a good grasp on what needs to happen.	Community formulated: People are by nature social animals who seek and enjoy working with others.	Rotate leadership and manage key organizational decisions by inviting participation by all members of the organization into the process.
You don't manage peers; you cooperate with them.	Equitable: Distributing the organization's resources more equitably in the organization will generate far greater returns to everyone in the long run.	Communicate throughout the organization honestly and truthfully.

Even when companies come to realize that rank-based leadership creates unhealthy and unprofitable organizations, they continue it. This always surprised me until I discovered the underlying paradigm that leads us to believe that there is no other way—the myth of leadership. We still need to learn how to create peer-based organizations that reject this myth and implement peer-based thinking. To help accomplish this, we will build on our last insight into four basic types of organizational attractors, beginning with the Big Chief and hierarchical organizations.

CHAPTER 5

"BIG CHIEF" AND HIERARCHICAL RANK-BASED ORGANIZATIONS

*Now one of the first requirements for a man who is fit to handle
pig iron as a regular occupation is that he shall be so stupid and
so phlegmatic that he more nearly resembles in his mental
makeup the ox than any other type. In our scheme, we do not
ask for the initiative of our men. All we want them is to obey
orders we give them, do what we say, and do it quick.*
—Frederick Winslow Taylor,
The Principles of Scientific Management

A global company that had recently experienced some traumatic change hired me to come in and facilitate some change management sessions. I held the first session with their accounting department. In the room were about thirty individuals, including the VP of finance and the accounting department supervisor. I began by asking them to share their thoughts on the recent changes. No one said a thing—complete silence. I shuffled my feet, looked over nervously at the VP, and asked again. They were all looking at me, but no lips were moving. Finally, the VP spoke up and began to explain the rationale behind the changes and why they were best for the company. The supervisor chimed in and scolded the group for not being supportive of the changes, which, by the way, had included letting go about half of the accounting department. The employees in the room began to look at me with some hostility in their eyes. In that moment, I saw the rank-based culture of that organization, and I realized that I had made a big mistake.

I recovered by calling for a break. During the break, I told the VP and accounting supervisor I would probably get better participation if they left the room. They reluctantly agreed, and I called the session back together without the two leaders. Boy, what an explosion of feelings went off in that room! They first chewed me out for having invited their leaders to attend, but then they unloaded on me all their pent-up frustration about having worked for years in a repressive, rank-based organization. For over two hours, they shared with me the history of their work experience, which I'm certain had not been all bad—but that's how they were remembering it now.

DEVELOPMENT OF A RANK-BASED ORGANIZATION

Some of them had been with the company since it was a start-up. The founder, a very bright and charismatic fellow, held tight control of all decision making and expected absolute loyalty. He was tough to work for, but had great vision, and they thought because the work was exciting that they could overlook his command-and-control personality. The company grew very fast, and soon it was too much for a single person to manage alone. So, the founder looked around and hired an executive team, who pretty much saw the world the same way he did—through the lens of the myth of leadership. They were all, however, very competent and used to giving orders, so they quickly imposed the right systems and structures on the growing business and growing number of employees. The company continued to do well in the roaring Internet boom of the 1990s.

Command and Control

The hidden problem, though, was that now instead of a single command-and-control personality sitting atop the company, there was an entire hierarchy of command-and-control personalities, all of whom felt they had the right to issue orders from above and get absolute loyalty from below. Communication began to suffer, as no one knew whom to trust, and little turf wars erupted between competing department heads. Information about business conditions and the state of the company became scarce and soon rumors were rampant. All of these factors caused a growing gap between reality and the rank-based leaders at the top of the company.

Effect on Productivity

Soon innovation and job satisfaction both began to disappear as the employees began to just put in their time at work while looking for jobs elsewhere. Even in a rank-based atmosphere they could survive as long as times were good. However, when difficult financial problems began to come up as the Internet bubble burst, the rank-based command-and-control responses of the senior executives undermined employee morale and productivity. The company's stock price was now in the penny stock range.

These employees were what Peter Drucker would call knowledge workers. Listening to these very dedicated and talented employees vent, I realized as never before that in the information/network economy, rank-based hierarchy could no longer be a successful form of organization. They had experienced their growth as a rank-based company, but now they were stalled both individually and as a company. In their hearts and minds, this group of bright and dedicated employees believed there had to be a better way.

TWO FORMS OF RANK-BASED ORGANIZATION

Organizations that lead with rank-based assumptions, logic, and practices—in a phrase, the myth of leadership—can take one of two forms. One is the charismatic and personal command-and-control style of a company in its early stages, where all power and authority seem to rest with a single individual, usually the founder/owner—I call this form the "Big Chief" organization. The other is the hierarchical command-and-control style of a more mature organization—I call this form the hierarchical organization. In either form, rank-based thinking dominates the organization, and the myth of leadership provides the justification for it.

The Big Chief Organization

In the start-up phase, or with small companies, control is centralized in one individual, frequently the entrepreneur (or entrepreneurs) who founded the company, and who occupies what is really the only position of unquestioned authority and power in the organization: the Big Chief. This entrepreneur will generally want to keep a tight rein on everything that happens and monopolize all decision making. Even if the entrepreneur wants to delegate authority, there is often no process in place to systematize and make such delegation effective.

Positions and jobs are created and dissolved on the fly, in an almost ad hoc manner as the company continually faces new and constantly changing situations. It is very difficult to find the time to create the integrated management structures that will be necessary for future growth. So it tends to be structured simply, with only a few well-defined roles and positions, and with little or no divisional and functional specialization.

The Hierarchical Organization

Hierarchical business organizations evolve naturally from Big Chief organizations. Power and control are still rank based and flow in only one direction, but now, instead of being administered by an individual, they are administered by a bureaucratic hierarchy. Not a lot changes in terms of understanding control, power, and management, but a corporate structure has emerged that can better handle the demands of the higher and more consistent flow of information through the organization. Even with a benevolent autocrat, given the expectations of unilateral power, most employees will adopt a strategy of compliance and make themselves dependent on their manager. These deliberate top-down, rank-based management structures are very time consuming. Yet, when business conditions are changing constantly, it's essential to respond quickly—something hierarchical organizations do very poorly. Both of these rank-based forms of organization produce characteristics that will produce failure in an information-based network economy.

CHARACTERISTICS OF RANK-BASED ORGANIZATIONS

There might be an infinite number of ways to design an organization, and many different models have been suggested—from the basic pyramid to the matrix to the lattice to the flattened organization. Yet, the most significant distinction, and most telling for the organization's long-term success, is whether it is a rank-based or peer-based organization. So, a factory, a bank, a high-tech company, and a government institution might have very different designs and organizational charts, but if they follow the logic and practices of the rank-based myth of leadership, they will, regardless of design, share in the same culture. This rank-based culture leads to inevitable consequences that are easily identified in most organizations today:

- Victim mentality—employees feel they have no role in decision making
- Entitlement—employees feel that management or the company owes them
- Cynicism and a lack of vision—employees see no connection between their work and the larger strategic goals of the organization
- Tradition valued more than innovation
- Constant crisis management
- Employee burnout
- Low trust between individuals and departments
- Competitive "CYA" attitude between interdependent groups or departments
- Inconsistent messages from management
- One-way, top-down communication
- Silo culture—turf protection and turf wars
- Failure to reward creativity
- Difficulty managing priorities and projects
- Bureaucratic rules and regulations that tend to stifle creativity and innovation

- Technology failures—systems and processes are broken and not repaired
- Loss of customers, suppliers, vendors, and more
- Loss of key people; brain drain

These consequences were all in evidence at the company where I was consulting—resulting in decreased productivity and higher costs, which added up to lower profitability. Unfortunately, because many of this company's leaders believed in the myth of leadership, they were taking actions that just made the situation worse. The root problems and solutions were obvious to the rank-and-file employees I spoke with, but due to the rank-based thinking of senior management, no one was listening.

What I've discovered consulting with and training hundreds of employees with dozens of different organizations is a real desire on the part of the employees to make significant contributions. We all share in a desire to make contributions and be recognized for them. We all want a feeling of self-worth. Many organizations are structured to make this nearly impossible, resulting in consequences like those listed above.

Solutions to the problems addressed by senior management are often known by employees further down in rank. But because of the assumptions of the myth of leadership, including rank-based logic and rank-based practices, no effective avenue exists for feedback to go up the hierarchy. As mentioned earlier, genuine communication will only occur between peers. Leaders, by virtue of possessing a "superior" position, are prone to assume also that they possess superior wisdom and insight. This attitude, one produced by the myth of leadership, has dominated business and other organizations throughout history. Perhaps reviewing this history will be helpful in both recognizing rank-based thinking in our own organizations and replacing it with peer-based thinking.

THE BIG CHIEF ORGANIZATION
IN HISTORY

If we were to trace the existence of the Big Chief organization through history, we would find it with the clan leader in the Paleolithic band, with the tribal chief in the Neolithic village, with the emperors and kings ruling classical cities, with the feudal lords in the European Middle Ages, with the traders and merchants during the rise of mercantilism, and with the factory owners and robber barons in the Industrial Revolution, right up to the entrepreneurs of start-up companies and small businesses today. The dominance of the Big Chief organization in business, however, ended around 1900, when the complexity of most businesses and the business environment rose to such a high level that more integrated managerial structures were required to support them.

The large corporations that gained monopoly power prior to this period were for the most part still managed by the men who founded them, hence were still controlled as a rank-based Big Chief organization with little or no significant integrated managerial structures. Vanderbilt, for instance, in his heyday personally oversaw the more than one hundred vessels in his fleet, controlled all his railroads, and, amid all his other business dealings, did his own bookkeeping. It is said that his own son hadn't a clue as to his father's management methods.

However, these corporations were beginning to grow larger than a single individual could manage. So, the maturing of the Second Industrial Revolution in the 1890s saw the rise of managerial capitalism with its class of professional managers and the hierarchical organization. It also witnessed the shift from the dominance of Big Chief organizations over business and a more oligarchic economy to where the dominant organization of the next one hundred years would be the hierarchical organization in a managerial capitalist economy.

BIG CHIEF ORGANIZATIONS TODAY

Today, Big Chief organizations are primarily seen in start-up companies and with small business owners. Some of these small businesses desire to remain small, while others desire to grow larger. This discussion will emphasize the latter type. Big Chief organizations are all characterized by the same properties. Though perhaps rich in intellectual capital, energy flow into the company in the form of money and information tends to be either overwhelming in its abundance or terrifying in its absence. Even worse, the company might be information rich but cash poor, or cash rich and information poor—in any case, the circulation rate of energy within the organization is low, static, inconsistent, or all three. It does not possess a complex-enough structure to help moderate and control the energy flow, which is not consistently high enough to allow more complex management structures to emerge.

When growth is substantial enough for managerial systems and structures to emerge, the entrepreneurial founder or leader, the Big Chief, must be willing to let go of control and step aside to allow the integrated managerial structures to emerge. Only in this way can the organization jump the threshold to a more sustained type of organizational activity.

Big Chief organizations need to establish the following types of integrated systems:

- People systems, including management, communication, and reporting systems
- Reward systems, including all compensation systems for pay, benefits, and bonuses
- Work systems, including economic strategy, market environment, and tactical systems

---

YAHOO, INC.

An excellent example of the successful transition from a Big Chief to a hierarchical organization is the Internet company Yahoo and its bright young founders, Jerry Yang and David Filo. Yang told *Fortune* ("Capitalist Century" 2000) that he did not really feel qualified to run Yahoo: "'People always ask me why I took myself out of the day-to-day operating responsibility. . . . But that's never what I wanted to do, and besides, I knew so little about business that I didn't want to slow things down when the company began to scale up.'" (F-81)

- Technology systems, including all the support and accounting systems required to run and sustain a company

When these systems are in place, growth can be better supported and sustained, and the future of the organization is more secure. Of course, when most companies make the transition from a Big Chief to a hierarchical organization, they carry over with them the rank-based thinking of the myth of leadership. The negative effects can be ignored for quite some time if the organization remains successful, but the negative effects won't go away, and the organization will eventually have to face them. This is precisely what was happening to the company I was consulting for.

THE HIERARCHICAL ORGANIZATION IN HISTORY

The twentieth century witnessed the emergence of bureaucratic managerial hierarchies from Big Chief organizations. Business conditions, including new technologies and production methods, increased the complexity of the business environments so much that large corporations were forced into becoming hierarchical organizations. Military and religious organizations possessed hierarchical structures prior to this, but the Big Chief mentality dominated, without any consistent managerial roles. It was the relatively recent invention of bureaucracy that gave modern hierarchical organizations their distinct structure and their new managerial mind-set.

Frederick Winslow Taylor

In 1911, Frederick W. Taylor published *The Principles of Scientific Management*, a monumental text that almost by itself created the managerial business enterprise. Borrowing the empirical method from science, Taylor and others applied observation, classification, and measurement of work to management and created the perfect mechanistic organization. Despite the inaccuracies of the Newtonian-Cartesian scientific worldview and the management model it inspired, we must not fail to appreciate the incredible progress that was made possible by Newton's achievement in science and Taylor's achievement in business management.

The hierarchical structure of business organizations was not a mistake based on faulty science, but rather the natural next phase of organizational life given the increased energy flow and complexity of the industrial revolution. Of course, what was to cause problems was the myth of leadership gaining wide acceptance at the same time. But to call Newton's scientific breakthrough dogmatic and repressive, as some people do, completely misreads the history of both science and culture.

Pyramidal Shape

Nevertheless, today most companies have a pyramidal organizational chart. They're built up from functionally oriented work groups such as sales, manufacturing, finance, human resources, and so forth. Superimposed on these functional specialties might be some type of matrix command structure based on individual products, strategic business units, or geography. Usually a functional dominance prevails, which has the tendency to create walls between people in companies, along with boundaries and chronic conflict. Nevertheless, many people feel safe working in a hierarchy—it is an organizational form that seems to offer great security and comfort. In the hierarchical organization we're told what to do, so individually the risk level appears low. In many ways, though, even the CEO isn't really free. The dynamics of the whole overwhelm the agency of the parts, even the "executive" parts.

Slow-Moving Hierarchies

Even a leader with good intentions will be trumped by the system if she doesn't understand it. Attempting to delegate some aspect of decision making to others or to a team without understanding the systems and processes of rank-based thinking will lead the manager to act in a way that nullifies the prior act of delegation. While teamwork is effective here, teams will not function very well within the hierarchical organization. Even with a benevolent autocrat, given the expectations of unilateral power, most employees will adopt a strategy of compliance and make themselves dependent on their manager. This makes deliberate top-down, rank-based management structures very time consuming at a time when business conditions necessitate quick responses.

ALFRED SLOAN AND
THE HIERARCHICAL ORGANIZATION

Alfred P. Sloan Jr., in his twenty-three years as president of GM, explored and mastered this form of organizational relations better than anyone. From 1923 to 1946, Sloan showed how to put together and run a business with the modern corporate structure of hierarchy organized by divisions, job specializations, corporate offices, unity of command, and standardized procedures. His success made hierarchical corporate structure the unquestioned way to organize a business. Simply put, he divided the corporation into two functionally distinct parts, the corporate office and the operation unit. The corporate office became the brain, and the operating unit, which could be multiplied as needed, became the body. The brain did the thinking and set the course, and the body stayed the course, ideally without thinking—all in accord with Taylor's management principles. Given the business conditions of the thirties, forties, and fifties, rank-based, autocratic management was marvelously successful.

Trouble with Unions

However, Sloan, along with other hierarchical managers of this period, had great problems dealing with unions. This conflict had several causes, but one key cause was the rank-based assumptions of the myth of leadership that guided the managerial decision making of the emerging large corporations. Because hierarchy and rank-based corporate structures subordinate the many to the few and grant what could appear to be excessive privileges to a few, they require constant validation of their position and policy. One way to do this is by appealing to the myth of leadership.

Aura of Legitimacy

The appearance of moral authority and even a sacred aura at the top of the hierarchy is essential to sustain the privileges of leadership. This need to establish and constantly reinforce the legitimacy of rank-based leadership requires that the myth of leadership be strongly supported by those in authority. If the majority of individuals in the organization do not acquiesce to the myth, the position and privilege of those at the top cannot be maintained without force. For these reasons hierarchy can create frequent conflict between labor and management.

RESISTANCE TO CHANGE

These rank-based hierarchies devote a lot of time and energy to resisting change and perpetuating relatively mechanical patterns of behavior through producing more negative than positive feedback. As someone once said, most organizations better represent their history than their promise. They fight hard to remain stable. This is natural. Any tendency to change is met with negative feedback. Companies work hard to survive.

Downsizing is one of today's most egregious ways for hierarchical companies to fight to stay alive. We need to understand and appreciate that, even knowing that these strategies don't usually work. A 1996 study by the American Management Association on corporate downsizing discovered that only 33 percent of corporate downsizers experienced productivity gains afterward, while 77 percent experienced significant drops in employee morale. More than half (53 percent) experienced a decrease or no increase in operating profits the following year.

Dynamics of Inertia

Hierarchies possess characteristics that at first make them successful in organizations. Their pyramidal shape provides stability and resiliency against any threats that might endanger them. With clear, integrated lines of command, they possess a negative feedback mechanism to quiet any internal disturbances or disruptions to the formalized systems and processes. In fact, in a hierarchical organization, change initiatives usually produce few or no results. This is not due to malevolent intentions on anyone's part, but to the dynamics of the whole. The negative feedback mechanism of the hierarchical structure, which makes it so successful, is so strong that it is always trying to attain equilibrium— any threats to stability or the status quo will be absorbed into the already existing systems and procedures.

Many hierarchical organizations enthusiastically embrace some new change initiative—perhaps involving a large investment of money—only to see no long-term results. After this happens a few times, people in the organization become cynical of the next "flavor of the month" program that comes along. Unfortunately, the failure of these programs is inevitable given the dynamic of the hierarchy, no matter how good the intentions of the people in it. So as a hierarchical organization gets bigger and bigger, or as the rate of energy circulation continues to increase, its very structure, which once was so beneficial, now causes the energy input to produce fewer and fewer returns. The more complex an organization gets, the greater its support costs become.

Decreasing Returns

In a hierarchical organization, these support costs—including the costs to continually legitimize the hierarchy, to control the hierarchy and keep it at equilibrium, to standardize procedures, and to maintain other auxiliary services supporting the hierarchy—continue to increase. These costs of hierarchy all continue to increase exponentially while the benefits of hierarchy increase incrementally. Businesses will frequently attempt quick remedies to cover up decreasing returns. Layoffs, mega-acquisitions, and reorganization of the corporate hierarchy are just a few of the short-term solutions organizations attempt, but diminishing returns will always catch up with them.

Business organizations are problem-solving entities. However, as Arie De Geus (1997), former director at Shell International, has pointed out, the average life expectancy of all firms is about twelve and a half years—so it seems that decreasing returns eventually undermine most rank-based businesses. A complex hierarchical organization must continuously increase investment just to maintain the status quo. Enlarging bureaucracy, increasing specialization, and spending more for communication are just some of the investments required. The problem with these investments is that they all become increasingly costly as benefits are reduced, making the organization increasingly vulnerable to collapse over time. As collapse nears, communication and control decrease, people interact less, and productivity drops off. When a complex hierarchical organization reaches this point, some organizational change is required to avoid complete collapse, being taken over, or losing parts of the company to invaders or other competitors. This was about the situation of the company with whom I was consulting. After speaking with several different employee groups, all of whom expressed the same frustration of working in a rank-based company, I had to report to the senior executives.

REPORTING TO THE EXECUTIVE TEAM

As I entered the conference room, I noted the presence of the CEO, CFO, COO, CIO, and the chief of staff—a lot of Big Chiefs. They had allotted me only ten minutes on their agenda. I had the impression they did not consider my project to be of much importance. After all, to rank-based leaders, collecting feedback from their rank-and-file employees is more a matter of appearance—give them the impression you're doing something to address their worries while continuing to disregard their concerns, hoping that they'll eventually disappear.

My intent was to show how their direct reports at practically every level felt frustration at not being given the opportunity to participate in decision making. I began by sharing the assumptions of the myth of leadership and the other aspects of rank-based thinking—the leadership mentality that was sabotaging the success of their company. Before I could say much, I was stopped by the COO, who loudly proclaimed that employees had no right to participate in any meaningful decisions, and they, the leaders, had no obligation to give them any. "People will whine, always have, always will," he said. Several other executives nodded their head in agreement.

I was shocked. All of the feedback and ideas I had collected were in that moment rendered meaningless, as I realized these executives would simply classify them as the inevitable complaints of unmotivated workers stung by "tough" leadership decisions. With a wave of his hand, the COO had dismissed the cares, concerns, hopes, and dreams of the employees of his company. He was the leader who gave the orders, and they were the followers who only had to obey. Simple as that, in his mind.

My ten minutes was up, and I felt like a complete failure. I had let down hundreds of employees of that company, whom I had come to care about. But all was not lost. Later that day, the CEO called me into his office and told me he agreed with what I had been trying to say. He also believed that a peer-based organization would unleash the dedication and innovation of his employees and lead them to greater profitability. He wanted to move in that direction and he enlisted my support. We both realized that he and I were alone in this desire—the other senior executives were (and would remain) entrenched in their rank-based ways.

CONCLUSION

Rank-based leadership was useful, even if not very healthy or meaningful, for a vast majority of organizations in the past because the complexity of their social and business environments was low. Now, however, our social and business environments are experiencing turbulent and ever-increasing complexity. Whether we call it the new economy of knowledge workers, the information age, or even the network society, what is clear is that in this environment, rank-based leadership does not provide the most effective and profitable way to manage an organization. It has reached its logical limit and no longer supports organizations well. The tide is inevitably turning against rank-based organizations managed under the myth of leadership. Organizations need to create a culture where everyone desires, and is able, to do their best to achieve outstanding results for the company. They need to become peer-based organizations.

When one or more companies can make this transition to peer-based thinking, other competitors will be left behind. Businesses need to further distribute decision-making power and practice participatory management. Of course, that will require a shift in the mental maps or models of the organizational participants toward peer-based thinking. Chapter 6 addresses this challenge.

PART THREE

CREATING AND
MANAGING
PEER-BASED
ORGANIZATIONS

CHAPTER 6

CREATING PEER-BASED ORGANIZATIONS

Instituting real team work means encouraging everyone's ideas and treating all members of the team as equals, and companies need to organize and empower teams of employees in which no knowledge ranks higher than another; each is judged by its contribution to the common task rather than by any inherent superiority or inferiority. . . . The modern organization cannot be an organization of boss and subordinate.

—Peter Drucker, "The Coming of the New Organization"

We have been comparing and contrasting the two basic paradigms of managing work, organizing companies, and relating to others—rank-based thinking versus peer-based thinking—along with their assumptions, logic, and practices. We have also explored the dynamic of the two types of rank-based organizations: the Big Chief and the hierarchical organization. If an organization can make it from the Big Chief stage to the hierarchical stage, it achieves a certain stability. This success, however, becomes the cause of future failure, as the hierarchical structure that brings stability will more often than not be protected by the rank-based thinking underlying the myth of leadership.

As change and uncertainty increase and as knowledge workers demand more meaningful work, rank-based leaders will be hard-pressed to sustain viable organizations. In its declining state, the rank-based organization will either attempt to survive through massive layoffs or by acquiring other companies and cannibalizing their resources, or it will be acquired or go out of business. As we move into the complex business environment of the network society, rank-based thinking will fail to achieve the required resiliency and creativity to prosper. However, an organization does not have to remain reactive to the ever-increasing changes in the business environment of the network society.

CONDITIONS FOR BECOMING PEER BASED

An organization can proactively gain the benefit of more productive and meaningful relationships by becoming peer based. Requirements for accomplishing this include the following:

- Ensuring that peer-based thinking becomes the common culture of the organization

- Structuring the organization in a way that promotes peer-based thinking

- Making changes in a way that is not too disruptive, thus avoiding generating a lot of resistance

- Tying the changes into the important areas of organizational decision making

In many ways the changes needed to become a peer-based organization must come from within the organization, not imposed from without. The employees themselves need to be co-creators of the new design, and there is no single right way of doing so. This requires that management not attempt external, rank-based coercion that completely disrupts current operations, but rather adopt methods that allow the gradual emergence of a peer-based culture. They must also ensure that these changes do not become just another management gimmick, but rather authentic changes in the way power and authority are exercised in the organization. Let's examine how this can be done.

PEER-BASED THINKING

Peer-based thinking does not mean we are all interchangeable, or that we are all the same—with equal talents, needs, ambitions, and so forth—or that we even make equal contributions. But what it does assert is that all members of the organization have equal standing. By this I mean everyone in the organization is given the opportunity to participate in decision making. It is a strategic principle guaranteeing that the organization will be more successful. By denying no one the chance to make decisions about issues affecting his or her work, it increases everyone's productivity and lowers costs. Peer-based organizations are based on the belief that the potential for growth is not primarily found in top management, but in the employees at every level of the organization. So we need to transfer power and responsibility to them. This does not mean, though, that anything goes, or that anyone can do whatever they please.

Power and Responsibility

Kurt Lewin, Ronald Lippett, and Ralph White (1939) conducted research with some teenagers at a boys' club that demonstrated how different leadership approaches to the exercise of power affected group behavior and the sense of group responsibility. Again, it is another example of how a group's behavior is more a function of context than of the character of the individuals who make up the group. They used three distinct leadership styles:

- Autocratic
- Democratic
- Laissez-faire

As autocratic leaders, they essentially set all the goals and made all the decisions, ordering the boys to do whatever they, the leaders, wanted and then criticized the boys' work. This, of course, is basically rank-based practice. The result was a hostile workforce in which the boys argued and fought with each other and with the "leaders." The boys, under the autocratic leader, were more likely to take advantage of one another and sabotage each other's work, while taking no responsibility for the results.

As democratic leaders, they facilitated the boys' own decision making and goal setting and nurtured mutual feedback regarding results and efforts. This, of course, is close to what I am calling peer-based practice. With this peer-based style, the boys showed more initiative and productivity as well as spontaneous cooperation and individual and group responsibility.

As laissez-faire leaders, they allowed the boys to do whatever they wanted without input or discussion of some common objective. The boys showed less direction and focus than under either of the other leadership styles. The laissez-faire leadership style could possibly be mistaken for peer-based management, but the two should be clearly distinguishable.

Peer-Based Management vs. Laissez-Faire Leadership

I want to stress that peer-based management is not laissez-faire leadership. As I have shared the promise of peer-based organizations with many different students of organizational theory, many of them assume that peer-based thinking will lead to chaos and directionless organizations. These associates make assumptions based on a false dichotomy: either you have a Big Chief at the top who is responsible for all decision making or a mob mentality where everyone does their own thing. To adequately respond to the legitimate concern that dichotomy expresses, we need to review what many management experts consider the seven key functions of organizational leadership, as listed below:

- To define the goals and strategic objectives of the organization
- To marshal and allocate organizational resources
- To organize, schedule, and deploy the work
- To monitor performance
- To motivate
- To communicate
- To develop people

Of course, classical leadership supported by the myth of leadership is autocratic. Rank-based leaders essentially make all the decisions in these seven areas and tell their direct reports what they will do. Laissez-faire leadership would fail to pay any attention to these key functions and hope they somehow get taken care of. Peer thinking, on the other hand, recognizes the need to perform these seven leadership functions and to create processes for making the decisions required, but in a way that invites participation from everyone in the organization. As Lewin et al. point out, "We are likely to modify our own behavior when we participate in problem analysis and solution and likely to carry out decisions we have made" (85). You may find it useful here to review the key assumptions, logic, and practices of peer-based thinking described in table 5 (pp. 76–77).

Conclusions from Lewin's Research

Two things stand out in Lewin's experiment at the boys' club on power and responsibility. The first is the different ways the boys responded when the leader left the room. In the autocratic context, the boys goofed off and bothered the weaker members. In the laissez-faire context, the boys stopped working and grew bored and restless. In the democratic context, the boys continued their projects, hardly noticing that the leader was not present. Obviously, only the democratic leadership context created true empowerment.

The second is how quickly the boys changed behavior when the management thinking was changed. Again, same boys, no sudden transformation in temperament—but in a different context very different behaviors and levels of responsibility emerged. For instance, when a democratic leader replaced the autocratic leader, the group of boys soon became more open, cooperative, and focused. Lewin, however, did remark that the transition from an autocratic group to a democratic group was much more difficult than any of the other changes. It seems that democratic behavior is more active and must be learned, while following the dictates of an autocratic leader is a very passive response and hence easier to develop.

The conclusion we can infer from these two observations is the need to design the organization in such a way that peer-based thinking will emerge naturally and be promoted by this very design. This must be done in accord with the other conditions already mentioned: (1) do not make it too disruptive and (2) tie the changes into the important areas of organizational decision making. Of course, most change initiatives I have observed are catastrophically disruptive and fail to make much of a dent in organizational decision-making processes. There is no real sharing of power, and rank-based thinking is never challenged. This must be avoided as we design organizations to promote peer-based thinking.

DESIGNING FOR PEERS—PEER LEADERSHIP COUNCILS AND TASK FORCES

You don't want to go out and make a radical change in your organizational structure to create a peer-based organization. This will damage all the informal but efficient networks that employees already have put together, ones that you'll want to leverage. It will also create tremendous resistance. By creating a peer-based organization without disrupting work or informal relationships, you gain credibility and momentum. However, if you do not genuinely share decision-making power and authority, you will not gain the passion and participation of your employees.

Three management vehicles are needed to begin a peer-based organization:

- Peer-based leadership councils—decision-making and cross-functional bodies of peers

- Task forces—teams chartered by the peer councils

- Senior executives—in the short term, the traditional management positions in the hierarchical organization

Let's look at each in turn.

Peer-Based Leadership Councils

Using the functions of management as a guide, we need to charter councils as either formal or informal review and decision-making bodies of cross-functional, cross-rank participants. Councils are formed, then, by bringing together people from every rank and department of the organization. Councils tap into the intelligence that exists throughout the company at every level. They require the involvement of all individuals, regardless of reporting structure. In a council, there is no rank; everyone comes together as peers—from the CEO to the front-line worker. Giving all participants input into decision making allows the best possible decisions to be made. Networks of councils will start to replace individuals and individual positions as key centers of authority and decision-making power.

The form of peer leadership councils itself capitalizes on the heart and intelligence of all employees. The more individual employees participate in decision making, the more their energy and dedication are enlisted. Given a share in business deliberations, individual employees expand their range of interests beyond narrow self-calculation to include a disciplined concern for the well-being of the whole organization. Unfortunately, today's predominantly rank-based hierarchical companies discourage the average individual's participation in decision making and so miss out on the wisdom and insight that exist at lower levels of the rank-based organization.

Task Forces

Peter Drucker, in his essay for the *Harvard Business Review* (1998), said of the coming organization, "Work will be done by specialists brought together in task forces that cut across traditional departments" (1). In hierarchical, rank-based organizations the design is typically functionally organized departments and interdepartmental teams all under the direction of rank-based leaders. The design for the new company, the peer-based organization, includes cross-departmental councils and task forces organized around customer needs and wants. They will all be under the direction of peer leadership councils composed of employees from every level and department of the organization. The task forces are responsible for doing the work, making task and process decisions directly affecting their work, and essentially executing the organizational strategy in contact with operational issues and customers.

They are chartered by the peer councils to carry out the crucial organizational tasks within the delivery of an organization's product and/or services to all stakeholders. There are many excellent books on building successful teams, so I will not elaborate on the dynamics of teams, or, as I am calling them following Drucker's lead, task forces. What I am describing instead are methods to allow these councils to operate more fully and effectively, freed from the constraints of rank-based thinking. Of course, what has been said to this point changes the role of all rank-based, hierarchical positions of leadership and especially that of senior executives. The major responsibilities of senior executives and other rank-based managers now include consulting, mentoring, questioning, and, by rotating through the councils and task forces, cross-fertilizing ideas and best practices. The peer councils' responsibilities include teaching and training the task forces they charter to do the work.

Senior Executives

In a peer-based organization, the former rank-based executives and managers, now as senior "leaders," perform four key functions. These new functions place them primarily in an advisory role to the organization, where their experience and knowledge can be best utilized.

- **Setting the general direction of the organization.** Senior executives oversee the company's strategic vision, values, and core competencies and advise all peer councils. They serve as a resource to the councils, functioning as teachers of corporate culture and values and as guardians of the organization's goals and vision. They create and manage the boundaries and link the councils together.

- **Acting as consultants to the councils and task forces.** Senior executives mentor the peer councils and task forces, sharing ideas, cross-fertilizing best practices, and helping to coordinate efforts. As they rotate through the different councils and task forces practicing peer-based thinking, they are uniquely positioned to generate energy flow within the company, leading to increased creativity and innovation. They allow the councils and task forces to make the decisions and to do the work.

- **Ensuring that the right questions are asked.** Senior executives do not monopolize decision making; in fact, most decisions are made in the councils and task forces. They are not the central authority, because there isn't one. They do need to measure progress and hold councils accountable for meeting their objectives. They let the councils know when they are off course and assist them in maintaining alignment with the whole. They do this by asking the right questions. They understand that power is not control and coercion, which only creates compliance and dependence, but rather influence, which generates commitment and interdependence.

- **Setting the conditions and providing the context for the task forces to be successful and to innovate.** The senior executives must teach the assumptions, logic, and practices of peer-based thinking to all members of the organization. The key to helping people to act properly is not values training, where you try to teach good habits or business ethics. The key is context. Create the context and conditions where people's better habits will emerge naturally. Design systems that encourage people to cooperate by creating the networks of councils and task forces as described.

Warning About Outside Experts

One practice to question carefully is the wholesale importing of outside consultants—with their myriad models and strategies—into the organization. Relying on consultants is a function of the myth of leadership. It is believing that not enough intellectual capital exists already in the company to successfully meet its challenges—when in fact the abilities and skills of most employees in companies are woefully underutilized, again due to the false assumptions of the myth of leadership. Further, adding to the lack of appreciation and underutilization of current employees is the hierarchical structure, which does not easily facilitate exchange of information and sharing of brain power.

In the process of mentoring and consulting with the peer councils and task forces in the open, generative environment of the peer-based organization, executives discover that the best strategies and models are home grown. As General George Patton (1949) said in his autobiography, "Never tell people how to do things. Tell them what to do, and they will surprise you with their ingenuity" (357). Further, now that senior executives have the key responsibility of being the consultants to the organization, there will be only the exceptional need to bring in outside consultants. When you trust your people and seek to consult them, not control them, and when you trust the intellectual capital already in the organization and do not import advice, then you are cooperating with the self-organizing dynamic in organizations. An outline of this division of labor between senior executives, peer councils, and task forces is shown in table 6.

People will productively work together and cooperate when they share common goals, receive proper information, develop the skill sets, and are able to recognize, utilize, and balance each other's strengths and weaknesses. This is the effect of the peer leadership councils in a

TABLE 6: THE MANAGEMENT OF PEER-BASED ORGANIZATIONS		
Senior Executives	**Peer Councils**	**Task Forces**
Set the general purpose and objectives of the organization.	Clarify the organizational purpose via strategizing and prioritizing.	Make task and process decisions.
Serve as consultants to the councils and task forces.	Clarify the organization's objectives via goal setting.	Do the work; perform from self-motivation.
Ensure that the right questions are asked.	Marshal and allocate resources.	Execute the organizational strategy at each level.
Set the conditions and provide the context for the councils and task forces to be successful and to innovate.	Charter, organize, and deploy task forces.	
	Hold the task forces accountable via monitoring and tracking.	
	Coach and mentor the task forces.	
	Validate the task forces' decisions.	
	Develop people.	

peer-based organization. Still, you need to think about where the peer councils are chartered and in what management areas. It is clear that where before the senior executives made most of the key decisions and then had them carried out by the managers beneath them, now the peer leadership councils make the key decisions mentored by the senior executives and carried out by the task forces—which are always accountable to the peer councils.

THE STRATEGY DIAMOND

While in London doing some consulting for a high-tech company, I was thinking about what an organization would look like that did not buy into the myth of leadership. I sketched out a model for putting the peer-based organization together—what I now call the Strategy Diamond. The model is built around customer needs, not a company's functional specialization. I was also convinced that I had to find a way to introduce the peer-based organization into a rank-based company that was not too disruptive.

The Strategy Diamond, as shown in figure 1, provides a visual picture that can help separate an organization's structure from the decision-making responsibilities. The decision making should be based on mission, customer needs, and satisfying those needs, rather than on functions or divisions. In essence, this means that organizations should be designed around customers and company competencies rather than static functions and hierarchical rank. As will be shown, the Strategy Diamond gives us a method to introduce peer councils and task forces in a way that does not immediately eliminate the traditional hierarchy; thus it provides a less threatening entry into peer-based management. Being less disruptive, it will not generate the resistance and hostility that would doom the effort to transition to peer-based thinking before it even began.

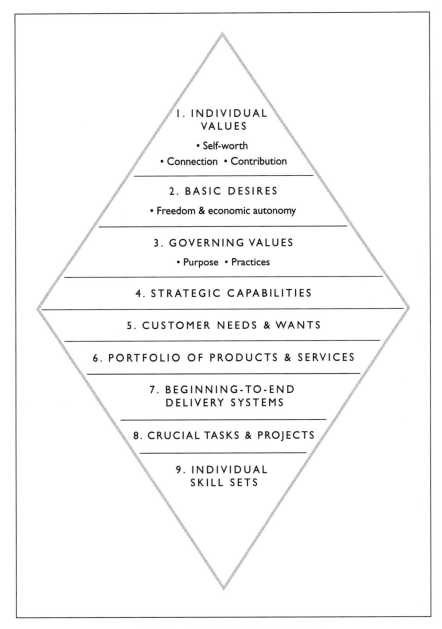

FIGURE I: THE STRATEGY DIAMOND

The Strategy Diamond has nine facets:

1. **Individual values.** All human beings share the same basic values, including the need for self-worth, connection, and contribution. Ultimately organizations exist to enable individuals to realize these values. The enduring organizations are those that accomplish this over the long term.

2. **Basic desires.** Across cultural and national boundaries, we also share the same basic desires, including the desire for freedom and security (more specifically, economic security). Enduring organizations are those that fulfill these basic desires, not so much for their customers as for their own employees.

3. **Governing values.** These include an organization's vision, mission, and core practices. A company must be clear on its sense of passionate purpose and its core practices for accomplishing that purpose.

4. **Strategic capabilities.** As perhaps the least understood of the organization's competencies, strategic capabilities can be determined by answering the question, "What is your competitive advantage in markets that gives you a sustainable edge over rivals?" or, "What do you do better than any rival that is hard to imitate and that adds value for your customers?"

5. **Customer needs and wants.** Following that analysis, a business must explore its customers' needs and wants, as well as those of noncustomers, and how they align with the company's own sense of purpose and its strategic capabilities.

6. **Portfolio of products and services.** When specific customer desires are matched up against the company's strategic capabilities, the company must decide strategically on what portfolio of products and services it needs to deliver.

7. **Beginning-to-end delivery systems.** Following that decision comes the full creation of each product and service, including research and development, product design, product manufacturing, assembly, processing, branding, marketing, selling, physical distribution, delivery to customers, and after-sales service.

8. **Crucial tasks and projects.** Within each delivery system are specific projects, tasks, and assignments required for successful functioning of the delivery system.

9. **Individual skill sets.** The final facet of the Strategy Diamond features the competencies, skills, and abilities of each employee needed for achieving results.

The Strategy Diamond enables us to envision peer-based organizations. Using this model we can create a full peer-based model like the one shown in figure 2. On the left side of the Strategy Diamond, we can now visualize organizational design and the managing of work through traditional management positions. On the right side, we visualize organizational governance through the peer-based leadership councils. (Specific types of peer councils are discussed in chapter 7.)

A rank-based organization tends to create a management structure and reporting lines wherein the senior executives place rank-based leaders such as EVPs over corporate divisions, VPs and directors over departments, managers over product lines, and team leaders over teams. Power and authority run in only one direction—from the top down—and reporting and accountability run from the bottom up. While this model can create a stable organization, it does not create a very innovative one. It possesses all the problems and negative characteristics of a rank-based organization that we have already discussed.

The Strategy Diamond, on the other hand, gives us a way to first visualize preserving the stability of the hierarchy while beginning to capture the creativity of the peer-based organization via the leadership councils. As mentioned earlier, a key condition of creating a peer-

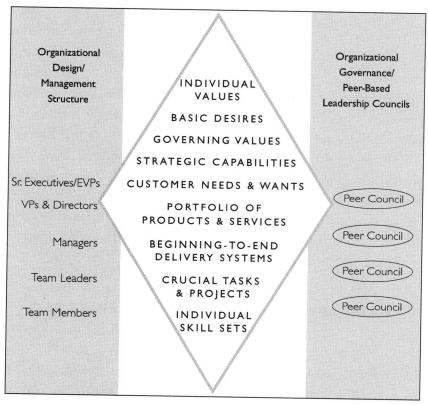

FIGURE 2: THE STRATEGY DIAMOND (PEER BASED)

based organization is that no radical changes should be made to the structure of the company. Instead, the executives and managers should begin creating networks of peer councils that they advise, consult, and train to become the key decision-making bodies.

An organization should feel free to experiment with the organizational design on the left side of the model; for instance, in deciding whether to structure the work of the company around geographical areas, customers, or products. In fact, by trying out different arrangements and occasionally restructuring, the organization creates deeper internal networks among the employees that serve to improve communication and flexibility.

Chartering peer-based leadership councils with appropriate training and coaching while keeping the traditional management structure
in place reduces the amount of resistance and confusion. Within a
short time, the organization will open up and begin to take on the
characteristics of a peer-based organization. As peer-based thinking
becomes common in the culture of the organization, the need for the
conventional management positions on the left side of the diamond
will disappear. Any major reengineering projects, however, even those
that would eliminate any "management position," should be introduced and led by the employees through the peer councils. Where
before the rank-based leaders made all the important decisions and
then had them carried out, now the peer-based leadership councils
make the key decisions with counsel from the senior executives.

BASIC DESIGN RULES OF A PEER-BASED
ORGANIZATION

In the peer-based Strategy Diamond model, with its clear separation of
reporting lines and decision-making authority, three basic rules apply:

- All decisions are made and conflicts resolved at the lowest possible level.
- The senior executives organize and mentor the peer councils.
- The peer councils organize the company's work at each particular level by chartering cross-functional task forces to perform the
  necessary work.

Decision Making and Conflict Resolution

Decisions should be made as close as possible to where the work is
being done. Rank-based organizations are instead set up to remove

decision making to the farthest point possible from the work locus, resulting in a growing gap between decision makers and reality. It is the sharing of decision making, not the abdication of power or responsibility, that results in empowering employees and makes centralization and decentralization happen at the same time.

In the peer-based organization, people are trusted to know what will work best at their level of the Strategy Diamond and they are empowered to organize the work there. In keeping with the increased freedom of decision making, these councils are responsible for deciding purchasing and pricing issues, for hiring and firing, for salary and compensation matters, and for establishing and monitoring team work rules and procedures. Access to information is crucial.

Senior Executives' Role

Senior executives charter the peer councils as decision-making bodies at key levels of the Strategy Diamond. Now, rather than making distant, top-down decisions, the executives move through the councils as mentors, consultants, and co-strategists, while each council makes the decisions within its purview. This allows information to be shared horizontally between councils and task forces and not be slowed, or perhaps even lost, in the climb up and then down a corporate hierarchy.

This distribution of information and control greatly enhances innovation and creative responsiveness to customer needs because decisions are made quickly by the people most knowledgeable about customer needs and desires. Further, recent research in neural networks by Efraim Turban and Jay Aronson (1997) shows that such distributed decision making is much more effective and, I believe, produces increasing returns where the marginal product grows faster than marginal costs. This approach does not create anarchy because the councils themselves are linked together through the sharing of some common members (the "link-pin" concept).

Peer Councils' Role

In practical terms, councils are responsible for setting up, teaching, and mentoring task forces, while the task forces do the real work. You could say that at the most basic level, decision making is done at the task force level with the support and mentoring of the respective councils. Leading through councils increasingly decentralizes decision making and satisfies the work motivators by giving employees greater control over their work. Such distributed decision making gives great incentive to innovate at all levels of the organization, thus increasing productivity and reducing costs. Councils are circular feedback systems of distributed decision making, and they are exceptionally creative and responsive to changes in business conditions in these turbulent times.

In his *Harvard Business Review* article, Drucker (1998) also describes the relationship between traditional departments and what I call peer councils and task forces:

> *Finally a good deal of work will be done differently in the information-based [peer-based] organization. Traditional departments will serve as guardians of standards, as centers for training and the assignment of specialists; they won't be where the work gets done. That will happen largely in task-focused teams.* (6)

In the peer-based organization, peer councils should have decision-making authority over

- Hiring, training, and retaining individuals with the right skill portfolios needed for the company

- Their own project teams
- Their own product/service lines
- The business units directed toward specific customers or geographies with the responsibility to allocate resources to the different business groups and units
- The business groups

CHARACTERISTICS OF PEER-BASED ORGANIZATIONS

Once we give up our egotistical attachment to rank-based concepts of managing, we can no longer justify our traditional leadership and supervisory positions and professions. This does not mean the important tasks of supervision are ignored or neglected—rather, they are redistributed throughout the peer-based organization to the cross-functional, and now rankless, councils and task forces. Key leadership functions will be exercised as well in peer-based organizations; however, they will be distributed through the peer council system as opposed to being identified with a hierarchical position in a rank-based organization. This leads to the following characteristics of a peer-based organization:

- Proactive mentality—employees feel they can make a difference
- Expectations not of entitlement, but of contribution
- Vision—everyone shares in strategic thinking
- Healthy balance between innovation and tradition
- Fewer crises and better work/life balance
- Everyone thinking and acting like an owner
- High levels of trust—because there are no secrets

- Willingness to admit "I don't know"—because there are no privileged elites
- Consistent, open, honest communication
- No communication barriers—everyone talks to everyone else as needed

In business organizations, these characteristics produce greater productivity and lower costs, which generate higher profitability.

CONCLUSION

As we have seen, to create a peer-based organization from a rank-based one requires four conditions. First, the individuals in the organization must reject the myth of leadership and make peer-based thinking the common culture. Second, the organization must promote peer-based thinking through its design of peer-based leadership councils where senior executives adopt the role of mentors and internal consultants. Third, the changes must not be too disruptive—using the Strategy Diamond model in preserving the old management structures while implementing peer-based thinking. Fourth, management must allow the peer councils to make the decisions in the seven key functions of leadership mentioned earlier (see p. 103).

A peer-based organization by my definition is one where participants have rejected the myth of leadership, practice peer-based thinking, and manage through peer-based leadership councils. There is no single best way to organize a peer-based company, and there will be as many different designs as there are for rank-based companies. No matter how it is ultimately organized, a peer-based organization will acquire competitive advantage over its rank-based rivals. In chapter 7, I discuss the strategy of peer-based thinking that makes this possible.

CHAPTER 7

THE STRATEGY OF PEER-BASED ORGANIZATIONS

We are all angels with only one wing
We can only fly while embracing each other.
—**Luciano de Crescenzo**

Each of us possesses amazing resources of knowledge, wisdom, and creativity. Our organizations need to learn to respect, nurture, and accommodate this wealth of human capital. We need to learn how to liberate the power of peers to create extraordinary organizations. Unfortunately, the way most companies are managed today, they fail to make use of their most valuable resource—their people. As we have seen, where the decision-making power rests with a select few at the top—the CEO and the executive team—the skills and abilities of most employees remain untapped. These corporate elites also tend to see the world in the same way and to share in a sense of entitlement over the organization's resources. History and current events show us that their interests do not always serve the best interests of the majority of people who have a stake in the well-being of their company.

This gap, I have argued, is a function of the context of rank-based organizations supported by the myth of leadership—the belief that those at the top of the hierarchy are somehow better, more intelligent, more worthy than those below them; that they are heroic individuals who deserve to command and control everyone else and reap huge monetary rewards as well. Today, however, there is too much information and too many choices for rank-based organizations—with their command-and-control hierarchies—to be successful. The workforce is too educated and possesses expectations too high to be satisfied by traditional rank-based job descriptions, which inevitably result in low morale, declining health, and lower productivity.

For some time, management experts have preached the importance of creating an empowered workforce. Yet, rank-based thinking keeps organizations and its people from achieving one. Trying to empower people while holding onto the myth of leadership is like trying to drive a car with one foot on the gas and the other on the brake!

THE CATCH-22 OF RANK-BASED MANAGEMENT

When I am conducting a workshop with corporate clients, especially if it is a change management workshop, I like to ask the participants to read the following quote and try to determine who said it as well as when it was said.

Every time we were beginning to form up into teams, we would be reorganized. I was to learn later in life that we tend to meet any new situation by reorganization . . . and a wonderful method it can be for creating the illusion of progress while producing confusion, inefficiency, and demoralization.

As it is the practice of rank-based organizations to mandate reorganizations from the top down, most participants assume the quote is quite recent. They are generally surprised to learn that this modern-sounding sentiment is actually attributed to the Roman scholar Gauis Petronius Arbiter, who died in 66 A.D. To me the quote speaks to our history of rank-based organizations and the pressing need to finally question and abandon rank-based management. Let's look at a modern example, a retail store in Utah, not far from where I live.

The corporate office had directed that their chain of several stores all undergo a major redesign of their store layout. None of the store managers—and of course none of the store employees—had been asked for input on either the need for the change in layout or the best way to carry it out in each store. Nor were they ever given any information on the reasons behind the decision to redesign or the larger vision of the corporate office. The managers were just told that this is what was going to happen. Outside experts were hired to study each store and then create the new design that the store manager would make happen. Throughout their examination and redesign of each store, the outside experts, like the corporate office, never solicited input from either the manager or the employees. When the redesigns were completed, the store managers were charged with implementing them, with a tight deadline. Naturally, the managers, in rank-based fashion, then passed this pressure down to their employees.

This example is not unusual, but rather typical of the way most organizations are managed. It also illustrates the three hallmarks of a rank-based organizational strategy:

- Decision making is not shared, but rather conducted at the top and imposed on those below

- The expertise of outsiders is privileged over the tacit knowledge and practical wisdom of employees
- Information is not shared, but rather tightly controlled on a need-to-know basis, where only bits and pieces are given to subordinates of the rank-based leaders

Negative Effects on Employees and Customers

The store employees, seeing the chaos of the store redesign and the anxiety on the face of their manager, grew anxious and stressed themselves. In the absence of any real information, they likely invented explanations that were far worse than reality. The heightened tension had the predictable result of less friendly customer service.

When rank-based managers monopolize decision making and information, employees experience a lack of control over their work life and will excuse themselves from taking any responsibility for results. In retail, this means they lose interest in trying to serve customers or to satisfy customer needs. So it should not be unexpected when sales in the store go down.

The Catch-22

The whole point of the store redesign was to increase profitability in each store. Corporate sees this as something that should motivate store managers, since manager bonuses are tied to store profitability. From the perspective of the corporate office, the store managers should be very grateful for the initiative taken by the home office. Unfortunately, the redesign was conducted in a typically rank-based fashion. The managers were told what they had to do without having input into the decision-making process and without sharing in any of the information that might have helped reduce their anxiety. Instead, corporate hired outside experts, thereby showing no confidence at all in their own managers.

From the managers' perspective, corporate's apparently arbitrary action made them feel insecure about their job performance and thus in their job position. Even though this was not what corporate had in mind, due to the lack of information sharing it was the inference drawn. Notice that there were no negative intentions anywhere in this process—from corporate to manager to store employee to customer— but it led to heightened stress and anxiety, lower productivity, and an inevitable decrease in profitability.

Corporate has told the managers, in effect: Do as we tell you— even though you had no part in the decision and were kept out of the information loop—and at the same time increase store profitability if you want your compensation to increase. The managers are thus confronted with a catch-22: If they do what they're told, they are unlikely to increase profitability; and if they don't do what they're told, they might improve store profitability, but they'll be putting their job in jeopardy. Either way, the outcomes are less than optimal. No wonder both managers and employees are feeling stressed and anxious, frustrated and dissatisfied.

The Peer-Based Alternative

The core belief behind peer-based organizations is that everyone from the CEO to the front-line worker has equal standing when it comes to information sharing and decision making. This, of course, requires a different mind-set from that of rank-based thinking, as illustrated by the three hallmarks of a peer-based organizational strategy:

- Decision making is shared, and all members are invited to participate at the level where they are most comfortable.

- The tacit knowledge and practical wisdom of employees are privileged over the expertise of outsiders.
- Information is shared throughout the organization.

Chapter 6 described how to design an organization that is not limited in its success by rank-based thinking and the myth of leadership. This chapter provides greater detail about how a peer-based organization, through genuine communication, gains competitive advantage over its rank-based rivals by using the three strategies described below:

- Peer-based councils
- "Diamond strength"
- Rotational leadership

THE STRATEGY OF
PEER-BASED COUNCILS

Today, work in the rank-based organization is frequently packaged as individual eight-hour-a-day, forty-hour-a-week positions filling specific job descriptions. The work offers minimal flexibility and freedom and fosters very little creativity. Feelings of entitlement abound due to the assumed permanency of static job positions, where success is measured by filling time, not getting results. Work is further organized into functional specialties with higher and lower levels and integrated into divisions in the rank-based company—an organization of work better suited to the factories of the nineteenth century than today's organizations. Furthermore, career success for members of the workforce is mistakenly measured by how far one climbs up the rank-based corporate ladder, not by how well one develops one's skills and competencies while meeting and exceeding customer needs.

The organization should be seen as a portfolio of goods and services, not as an assortment of jobs organized functionally and separated divisionally. Career success should be measured by results, not by one's ascendance on the ladder of rank-based positions. Management should be seen not as a permanent rank-based leadership position, but as a competency developed and practiced by each member of the organization. And managers should fulfill their role as promoter of cross-fertilization of ideas and best practices between councils and project task forces, not as agents of top-down command and control. Success, both organizationally and individually, needs to be measured by results meeting stakeholder needs, not by acquiring status. It is time for peer-based leadership councils.

The Goals of Peer Councils

When an organization charters peer councils, employees shed their hierarchical roles and begin to see things differently. People from all over the organization get to know one another and learn how to genuinely communicate. People work together productively and cooperate when they share common goals, receive proper information, have the required skill sets, and are able to recognize, utilize, and balance each other's strengths and weaknesses. Some of these necessary elements are generally missing in the rank-based organization, with its centralized authority and top-down command-and-control structure. In the absence of rank-based thinking, a greater sense of community is developed that fosters increased competency in all members of the organization. Peer councils provide the vehicle for this development, with the following goals:

- To foster a sense of equal standing and genuine communication among all employees

- To allow everyone in the organization to contribute to strategic thinking and decision making

- To ensure that everyone in the organization begins to think like an owner

- To provide everyone in the organization knowledge-based skills that do not become obsolete

In striving to achieve these goals, peer councils become multiple centers of decision-making authority and responsibility. By distributing power and responsibility throughout the organization, they tap into the whole intelligence and talent latent within the workforce, giving the organization comparative strength over rank-based rivals in a range of factors including those discussed below.

Rank-Based vs. Peer-Based Decision Making

Big Chief or hierarchical decision making might seem to be more expedient and efficient, and in some cases, might be. However, time saved by these types of decision making is often lost to correcting the inevitable mistakes that arise from the narrow range of vision of a single, rank-based decision maker. This is especially the case for complex situations and issues, where the inclusion of many different perspectives is not only helpful, but often necessary, to fully define the problem and identify solutions. With a limited perspective and lack of genuine information, the Big Chief must work with the given dynamics of the rank-based organization and cannot fully grasp the extent of the problem and nature of the solution. Rank-based decision making, however speedy, leads to more bad decisions. So, even where decision making in peer councils might take more time up front, though that is not necessarily the case, the many perspectives of council members shared in the decision-making process generate better problem identification and more effective problem solving. This saves time and resources in the long run.

Harmonizing with a More Conventional Organizational Structure

Companies can be structured in innumerable ways. For example, a company can be organized into different business groups, which represent customers' needs and wants divided either by industry, geographic region, or some mixture of both. The business groups can be further divided into business units, which represent the portfolio of products and services of the company delivered to each strategically focused customer group. Within each business unit are the delivery systems for products and services, each represented by a product or service line. Cross-functional and interdisciplinary project task forces are then organized to take care of the crucial assignments and tasks within the work flow of each product or service line. Finally, project task forces are composed of individual employees with their own sets of interests, skills, and competencies. This collection of parts forms the structure of a company, and as always, feedback and communication are crucial.

Within this structure, conventional, hierarchical reporting lines could be drawn as follows:

1. Individuals report to project task forces.

2. Project task forces report to a product line.

3. Product lines report to a business unit.

4. Business units report to a business group.

5. Business groups report to management.

Yet in the peer-based organization, the management of these reporting lines is not rank based, for each area is supervised not by a single rank-based leadership position, but by a peer council. This format allows for the stability of the familiar organizational structure and reporting lines, but adds the innovativeness of the peer councils. The scale and scope as well as variety of these peer councils depend on the unique needs of each individual organization.

Types of Peer Councils

In a peer-based organization, peer councils can be chartered to oversee all aspects of the organization. Following are a few of the many types of peer councils that could be chartered:

- *The company peer council* could oversee the company's strategic vision, values, and core competencies.

- *The business group peer council* could set the company's business objectives and make strategic market and product decisions by being attuned to the needs and desires of each group's customers. It would analyze future trends in business and key markets and design work structures and reporting lines at the business group level.

- *The business unit peer council* could oversee the geographic or industry sector focus for the entire portfolio of the company's products and services. It could make the necessary resource allocations for the various business units and design work structures and reporting lines at the business unit level.

- *The product line peer council* could make product line decisions, and oversee all product and process councils, within each business group. It could design work structures and reporting lines at the product line level. It could partner with major industry players by including them on their councils and task forces. It might oversee a specific product line or service and the related project task forces. The product/process councils make specific operational decisions within their respective product lines or processes, oversee the project task forces, and design work structures and reporting lines at the project task force level.

- *The employee skills council* could oversee individuals' portfolio of skills and competencies and ensure that all individuals within their function are meaningfully engaged on appropriate project teams. This council might make specific skill portfolio decisions—for example, what types of competencies and skills are needed—and oversee training and development of people in the organization. It could function as a service council to the business units.

Each council is responsible for ensuring the execution and accountability at its own level. Councils must practice patience, as opposed to surrendering to the quick-fix mentality. They must build trusting relationships, for true freedom requires trust. They must set clear role and goal expectations and identify where help and assistance can be obtained, as well as establish clear accountability. This should ensure the optimum use of everyone's talents.

Council Membership

Here are a few other thoughts to keep in mind in determining council membership:

- Councils should be organized across levels, functions, and rank.
- Key customers, clients, vendors, and stakeholders should be included on the councils.

- Council size should be determined by the exigencies of each particular organization.
- Some council memberships should be voluntary, while others should be chosen by council members.

Each council has the authority to charter cross-functional teams for specific projects at its level. There are no "leaders" in the councils, but rather facilitators, who plan and conduct the council meetings. In general, council facilitators should be voluntary positions and periodically rotated, with the expectation that every council member will have a turn in this position.

New Roles Mean New Titles

In the transition to becoming a peer-based organization, the single decision maker is replaced by councils and task forces—suggesting a change in titles. The CEO stays the CEO but is no longer the *chief*, but rather the *consulting*, executive officer. The same shift from "chief" to "consulting" might apply to other senior executives as well—for instance, the CFO might become the consulting financial officer, and so on. These new titles make clear their new role in an "open and leaderless" organization. Other title changes might occur as follows: the title of vice president might be changed to mentor; the title of director might be changed to facilitator; the title of manager might be changed to coordinator. These new titles reflect the change of culture from rank-based, top-down command-and-control management to a peer-based culture of equal standing.

Councils Must Be Peer Based

Chartering councils but failing to make them peer based, or not involving people from every level and function of the organization, is a big mistake. The first attempt I made at introducing councils was with a well-intentioned CEO of a company that was not performing as well as it might have. We chartered the councils in the critical decision-making areas of the company, but against my wishes no one below management level was allowed to participate on a council. The rank-based chain of command was left in place within the councils, so the organization essentially remained the same rank-based hierarchy it was before.

As I went around explaining the council model to different groups in the organization, they all were excited to have a part in the decision-making process. The idea of contributing to the organization's strategic vision and tactical execution was very motivating for them. This was a company of very bright employees, and most of their knowledge and most of their abilities were being wasted in the traditional typecasting of rank-based thinking—as reflected in statements such as "Your job is to develop what we tell you to develop and not to think about what or why" and "Your job is to market what the engineers give you."

The employees at every level of the company had good reasons to explain the company's relative lack of success, but their thinking was never solicited. They saw the councils as a possible way to finally make some impact on the success of their company, and so did I. But there was too much resistance from the senior executives, who did not want to give up power and privilege. The well-intentioned CEO was forced to compromise his vision and make the councils rank based. The Big Chiefs still monopolized all decision making and neglected the councils, which were only their traditional rank-based staff in any case, or used them as mere privileged "gofers." This in reality was the same rank-based model as before but with a different name.

The economic situation with this company did not improve. Although the rank-and-file employees would have made a tremendous difference, the rank-based leaders continued to ignore the willingness and ability of those beneath them in rank to assist in solving organizational problems. Soon the rank-based leaders themselves were replaced by the board of directors with other rank-based leaders, and the unfortunate saga continued.

THE FOUR KEY AREAS OF ORGANIZATIONAL DECISION MAKING

Issues of organizational management cannot be separated from an understanding of organizational strategy and design. Figure 3 shows the four key areas of organizational decision making:

- **Vision**—manifested in the organization's strategic direction
- **Culture**—manifested in the organization's people
- **Performance**—manifested in the organization's tactics
- **Results**—manifested in the organization's operations

Following a brief description, we'll see how each of these key areas can be aligned with a peer council chartered to leverage the competitive advantage possessed by peer-based organizations.

Vision—Strategic Direction

Strategic direction is determined with a thoughtful eye on the business horizon to create the vision of the organization. The foundation of competitive strategy is aligning an organization's strategic capabilities with the present and future needs and wants of both current and hoped-for customers. The fit between what an organization does best—its strategic capabilities—with what customers both need and want determines the strategic portfolio of products and services the organization should deliver. This clarifies the business horizon in

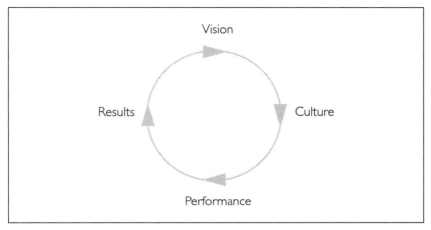

FIGURE 3: THE SUCCESS CYCLE

the sense that it lets the organization establish in which market segments it wants to acquire superiority in the near future. The following four questions can be of great help in establishing strategic direction (question 1 reveals strategic capabilities):[6]

1. What is your competitive advantage in markets that gives you a sustainable edge over rivals? That is, what is it that you do better than any rival, that is hard to imitate, and that creates value for the customer?

2. Who are your customers (including hoped-for customers), and what are their current and future needs?

3. Which products and services will you develop and support, and which not?

4. How will you contact and deliver to your customers?

6. Questions 2–4 were suggested by Michael Porter's 1996 essay "What Is Strategy?" *Harvard Business Review*, November–December).

Culture—People

For any strategy to be successful in the long run, first it must be aligned with the basic values and desires of all individuals who have a stake in the life of the organization and create a culture that values people. This includes not only customers and equity owners, but all employees, suppliers, and vendors as well. Luckily, we all share the same basic values and desires as described earlier: freedom and economic security plus a sense of self-worth, connection to something larger than ourselves, and making a contribution to others. This requires that the organization place a high value on open and honest communication. Everyone in the organization needs to have permission as well as the opportunity to talk to anyone else in the organization. This culture of openness and transparency needs to be fostered at all levels of the organization.

Performance—Tactics

After determining a strategic direction and developing the culture, an organization must focus its energy to engage rivals in the "intelligent clash of wills" in serving customers. Marshaling the troops to meet and defeat competitors through superior performance while creating value for customers is referred to as tactics. It brings the organization's strategic vision into clear focus in the present. It requires transparency and full knowledge of how each employee contributes to strategic and tactical success.

Results—Operations

Operations is where the rubber meets the road: doing the work and generating results. However, in competition and interaction with others, nothing ever goes as planned. Inevitably, the best strategy and tactical plans break down. Clausewitz, the Prussian military strategist, blamed this on the "fog and friction" of the intelligent clash of wills. So, in the actual performance of an organization's strategic and tactical plans, expect the unexpected. The key to operational effectiveness and success is competence in problem solving and decision making.

The interaction of these four areas of organizational decision making will determine the success or failure of the enterprise. Rank-based organizations have a very limited range of strategies in these four areas due to their limiting organizational decision making to the few rank-based leaders who share the same narrow perspective. It is human nature to define and fix problems in whatever way worked in the past. When conditions change, as they do today at an ever-accelerating pace, past solutions become future problems. Without multiple perspectives and experiences to draw on, rank-based leaders will apply ineffective, outdated solutions to newly evolved problems.

STRATEGY OF DIAMOND STRENGTH

Strategic thinking has tended to emphasize one of two things: either a company should strategically focus on its own core competencies, an inward focus, or it should focus on the business environment, an outward focus. The Strategy Diamond introduced in chapter 6 combines those two strategic elements. Now I want to tie it in with four key aspects of organizational strength and four key peer councils.

Four Key Aspects of Organizational Strength

The first column in table 7 reveals the strategic qualities of peer-based organizations.

TABLE 7: DIAMOND STRENGTH IN ORGANIZATIONS		
Four Key Aspects of Organizational Strength	**Four Key Peer-Based Leadership Councils**	**Four Key Areas of Organizational Decision Making**
Strategic alignment	Strategy council	Vision
Strategic openness	Functional council	Culture
Strategic transparency	Tactical council	Performance
Strategic competence	Operational council	Results

- *Strategic alignment* occurs when the organization's strategic capabilities, the wants and desires of the organization's customers, the actual portfolio of products and services provided by the organization, and the skill portfolios of all employees are aligned.

- *Strategic openness* occurs when feedback and communication involving strategy, tactics, and operations are allowed to flow in every direction, with few if any roadblocks, and anyone is free to communicate with anyone else in the organization.

- *Strategic transparency* occurs when all members of the organization are informed and understand the strategy and how what they do serves the customer and fits in with the organization's strategic direction.

- *Strategic competence* occurs when all members of the organization are allowed to develop their own unique expertise, to practice the skills of strategic thinking, and to act like an owner and be responsible for results.

Four Key Peer-Based Leadership Councils

The second column in table 7 includes four key peer councils—the strategy council, the functional council, the tactical council, and the operational council—whose responsibilities include overseeing the four key aspects of organizational strength.

- The *strategy council* continually reviews the organization's strategic capabilities along with present and future customer needs and wants to determine which products and services to offer to which customers. It views each facet of the Strategy Diamond from the perspective of vision and strategic direction and is responsible for ensuring that alignment is present in and between each facet to create and maintain competitive advantage in the marketplace.

- The *functional council* continually reviews how best to develop, reward, and compensate the organization's people. It views each facet from the perspective of culture and people and is responsible for ensuring that openness is present in and between each facet. The council monitors how well the organization is doing in satisfying all the stakeholders' basic needs and desires.

- The *tactical council* continually reviews how best to engage both customers and competitors—that is, how best to deliver products and services to customers and successfully execute business strategy. It views each facet from the perspective of performance and tactics and is responsible for ensuring that transparency is present in and between each facet.

- The *operational council* continually reviews how to do all of this more profitably. It views each facet from the perspective of results and operations and is responsible for ensuring that competence is present in and between each facet. It also stays watchful for "high-level dumb," a condition characterized by a large and growing gap between the beliefs of those at the top of the organization and the reality in the trenches. The council monitors and corrects any problems in communication within the organization and constantly looks for ways to improve operations and make them more efficient.

PEER-BASED STRATEGY

A peer-based organization, through its council model of decision making, generates more strategic, functional, tactical, and operational options for the organization. It has a greater ability to be flexible and respond in a more timely manner to changing market conditions. And it has a higher tolerance for ambiguity and uncertainty. Overall, an organization of peers brings out the best habits of all its employees.

Recently, I worked with a company whose young founder and president was sincerely committed to creating a peer-based organization. He invited me to come in and introduce the Strategy Diamond model along with some key training to improve decision-making and communication skills. As could be expected, the rank-and-file employees were very enthusiastic about the opportunity to participate in decision making as peers, while the senior executives—with the exception of the young president—were somewhat skeptical.

When I present the two paradigms of rank-based thinking and peer-based thinking, people recognize immediately what I'm talking about. They all have horror stories to tell about rank-based leaders who are great believers in the myth of leadership. Most appreciate hearing about the inevitable negative consequences of rank-based management and are inspired by the possibility of peer-based organizations. However, often they are not quite certain it will work.

We chartered the four key councils—the strategy council, the functional council, the tactical council, and the operational council—and each council chose its own facilitator. Because the company was small enough, each employee was able to be a member of each council. They were truly peer councils, as the founder and president participated as a peer, not the Big Chief. There was immediate enthusiasm within the company and a great sense of empowerment.

I mentored the first few council meetings and was excited by the participation and sharing of ideas from all council members. Even after the meetings, the cross-fertilization of ideas and conversation continued. During the first few weeks, I delivered training to the council facilitators on meeting management and consensus decision making. They in turn taught their councils. We planned further training in creative problem solving, conflict resolution, and communication so that each person in the organization would be able to develop his or her own skills and contribute as an equal partner in organizational decision making.

As I spoke with different employees, they shared similar feelings and experiences. They all felt more creative on the job, as well as more focused on their company's business model. The peer-based leadership councils had enabled them together to better clarify their organizational purpose, what was working, and what was not working. This gave them all a sense of ownership in the results of the company—a great motivation for finding ways individually and collectively to increase productivity and decrease expenses.

Practically speaking, what can people at different levels of a company do to help create a more peer-based organization? Whatever their level of responsibility, they can view their work from the perspective of strategy, tactics, operations, and people. They can then charter within their own team, department, division, or shop the peer councils made up of their direct reports and begin to operate like a peer-based organization in miniature. Each of these peer-based councils will have the responsibilities described above.

THE STRATEGY OF ROTATIONAL LEADERSHIP

Rotational leadership is a key strategy of peer-based organizations, where leading and managing are not permanent positions, but rather competencies in each employee's skill portfolio. Ultimately, leadership position should be based not on rank and seniority, but on passion and peer review. Rotating the leadership position on a regular basis is the most effective way to begin fostering peer-based organizations. Even in the absence of peer councils, rotating leadership positions on a regular basis will create soft hierarchies that give people a greater chance at participation and contribution. Also, the fact that people share in the ownership of leading means that they also share in the burden of communicating knowledge and information to others. This improves teamwork and knowledge sharing in a manner that makes organizations self-correcting. Three of the very successful organizations I mentioned earlier—W. L. Gore & Associates, the Orpheus Chamber Orchestra, and Ricardo Semler's Semco—practice in varying degrees this idea of rotational leadership.

The essence of rotational leadership is that those in management positions have defined term limits. Individuals in management positions are given a certain amount of time to fill their management assignment and select two or three specific and measurable objectives for their tenure. When their time is up, other individuals are chosen and the rotation continues. This keeps the energy flow through the organization generative, and makes possible a wider choice of strategic paths and a greater number of creative innovations. This practice also undermines any residue of the myth of leadership and allows everyone in the organization to develop their own potential to the fullest. Furthermore, it brings about greater equality in salaries and prohibits the excesses of executive pay. This boosts morale, trust, and productivity better than any leadership seminar or change initiative imposed on the organization and increases the competitive advantage of the organization over its rank-based counterparts.

In rank-based organizations dominated by the myth of leadership, strategizing and decision making are the job of the top executives, and they closely protect this right. The old guard, subconsciously or not, first and foremost want to preserve the stability and equilibrium of the organization, and so tend to create only very dull strategies. Giving leaders and managers term limits on their management assignment along with clear objectives for their term helps create an eternally fresh and energetic organization. Otherwise, there will continue to be a growing disaffection with corporate leadership—as Seifter and Economy (2001) point out as they contrast the tremendous success of rotating leaders at Orpheus with the traditional permanent leadership position.

Research by Carnegie Mellon business professor Robert Kelley has revealed widespread dissatisfaction with corporate leadership among employees. Forty percent of those surveyed believed that their bosses had questionable leadership abilities, and almost as many believed that their bosses had "ego problems" that made them feel threatened by and defensive around talented subordinates and new ideas. Less than half of all leaders inspired trust in their subordinates, and only one in seven was seen as a potential role model to emulate. When such shortcomings pervade a company, even otherwise credible leaders are undermined and followers feel adrift. (89)

CONCLUSION

The concept of the peer-based organization is based on a strategic principle, not a moral one. Those organizations that value and reward peer-based thinking will be more successful in acquiring and maintaining competitive advantage and so achieve strategic success. As we have seen, creating a peer-based organization does not mean doing away with management positions or management structure—work still needs to be managed. However, the governing leadership choices in the four key decision-making areas of strategy, tactics, operations, and people will be made not by the self-similar elites, but by councils of peers drawn from every level and function.

Indeed, today a higher consciousness is emerging in organizational thought that rejects rank as the chief element of organizing relationships. The new peer-based organization will only emerge on the periphery and eventually take over the center because corporate leaders at the center generally lack the courage and strength to dismantle their rank-based privileges. Change arising on the periphery has been the pattern for all evolutionary progress. It could happen at the center, if the majority of organizational members demanded it, but we lack sufficient historical precedent where this has occurred. The future belongs to peer-based organizations because individuals in these organizations behave more responsibly, more intelligently, more strategically, and more cooperatively than they would in traditional rank-based organizations.

Corporate governance must be reformed so that it rests not on the same old aristocratic class—whether the corporate board or executive teams—but with the employees of the company. Peer-based councils will make their organization more prosperous not only by being more creative, more flexible, and more dynamic, but also by being more internally and externally equitable and hence more socially responsible.

The myth of leadership sustains rank-based relationships and leads us to believe that there is no other way. In this chapter I have tried to show how to strategically design an organization that is not limited in its success by that myth. A peer-based organization is by definition one where participants have rejected the myth of leadership and practice peer-based thinking, where everyone in the organization has equal standing with respect to information and contribution to the decision-making process. There is not a single best way to organize a peer-based company, and there will be as many different designs as there are for rank-based companies.

Rank-based organizations are based on either the Big Chief or the hierarchical form of leadership. Peer-based organizations, on the other hand, use a very different model to become "open and leaderless." That is the topic of chapter 8.

CHAPTER 8

OPEN AND LEADERLESS
PEER-BASED ORGANIZATIONS

The coming century will be unfriendly to superhero CEOs who try to wing their companies heavenward by sheer force of will. Success will belong to companies that are leaderless.... In the 21st century, the all-powerful CEO may not be powerful at all. Companies that thrive will be "led" by people who understand that in business, as in nature, no one person can ever really be in control. —**John A. Byrne,** *BusinessWeek*

As we experience social relationships in the coming years, partnering and cooperating with others will contribute more to our success than dominating and controlling them. When hierarchy and rank as a social strategy are no longer effective, leadership will be replaced by true peer-based organizations. In the absence of rank-based leaders, the talent, vision, and creativity of all members of the organization will be required and so developed, practiced, valued, and rewarded.

Albert Einstein once said the most important question each person has to answer is whether this universe is a friendly place, a good place.

I have often thought about that question. Answer in the negative and you will attempt to control things. Answer in the affirmative and you discover that relationships and the organizations they constitute have a goodness and value all their own. The movement to peer-based, leaderless organizations is a part of the natural dynamic of developing human possibilities that is now beginning to be realized in the network society.

If people are trusted enough to be given the freedom to make decisions—and led not through rank-based, command-and-control practices, but through mentoring, strategic questioning, and genuine communication—then the organization will become peer based. This trust requires the set of assumptions we have already identified as peer-based thinking. Organizations operating in harmony with peer-based thinking will be characterized by openness, creativity, flexibility, resilience, and responsiveness.

TWO FORMS OF PEER-BASED ORGANIZATIONS

Just as organizations that lead with rank-based assumptions, logic, and practices can take on one of two forms—"Big Chief" and hierarchical—peer-based organizations assume one of two forms as well. Recall that with rank-based organizations there is the charismatic and personal command-and-control style of a Big Chief organization in its early stages, where all power and authority seems to rest with a single individual—the Big Chief, usually the founder/owner. Then there is the more impersonal command-and-control style of the more mature, hierarchical organization. In either case, rank-based thinking dominates the organization, and the myth of leadership provides the justification for it.

When rank-based thinking is rejected, the very nature of the organization changes. Although there is no one best way to organize a peer-based organization, we have discussed the importance of peer-based

TABLE 8: FORMS OF RANK- AND PEER-BASED ORGANIZATIONS	
Rank-Based Organization Forms	**Peer-Based Organization Forms**
Big Chief Organization	Open Organization
Hierarchical Organization	Leaderless Organization

thinking and managing through peer councils. Yet, based on inspiration from the attractors in chaos theory (see chapter 4), peer-based organizations begin as what I call "open" organizations and potentially evolve into true "leaderless" organizations, both of which are led by peer councils. (The forms for both rank-based and peer-based organizations are shown in table 8.)

The open organization retains some traditional management positions and structure, though no longer operating from rank-based thinking. These positions are preserved for stability and institutional memory reasons. The open organization therefore serves as an important transition stage between the hierarchical and the true leaderless organization. The executives in these positions, however, perform the functions of coaches and mentors, not key decision makers within the organization. The decision-making role is performed by the peer-based leadership councils. As these councils become better trained and experienced, the need for any traditional management positions will diminish until it disappears entirely.

At this point in the organization's evolution, true peer-based ways of managing organizational issues—the strange attractor of the leaderless organization—will emerge. I do not believe we can chart in advance exactly what this will look like, nor do I believe there are any such companies today. But it is exciting to think about. When all members of the organization are true peers, it will make no sense to call one member a leader and others the followers. The emergence of open and leaderless organizations will be aided by, though not dependent on, our growing network society. It might be helpful to look at networks and peer-based organizations together.

NETWORKS AND PEER-BASED ORGANIZATIONS

As discussed in Albert-László Barabási's book *Linked: The New Science of Networks* (2002), networks increase the degrees of freedom in a society or organization by increasing the possible number of paths that people can follow and explore. Even more so than hierarchies, networks are resilient. Unlike hierarchies, networks are also creative. These two traits, resiliency and creativity, make the network the most robust structure imaginable. A network is composed of content, nodes, and connections. The nodes and connections carry the content. Increasing the degrees of freedom increases the number of nodes, or centers of decision making, in a society or in an organization. This, in turn, leads to an increase in freedom. In organizational terms, then, you create information-rich networks by increasing the number of centers of decision making and connections in an organization. This will allow the organization to capture and leverage the robustness of networks.

How do you create these robust networks? As mentioned earlier, you do not want to make radical changes in structure too soon that will damage the informal alliances and networks that you will need to use later. The key to expanding networks is to set up cross-functional connections between an expanded number of nodes (decision-making centers) through the peer council system. As the number of networks in society increases—educating us all about the workings and benefits of interconnected nodes—the companies that can mirror networks in their own organization will become wildly successful. Peer councils increase the number and quality of centers of decision making through councils and so capture the resiliency and creativity of networks. Let's take a closer look at both forms of peer-based organizations, knowing that much of what we say is of necessity hypothetical.

THE OPEN ORGANIZATION

Strong believers in the myth of leadership refuse to distribute power and decision-making authority to others not of the same rank in the organization. For them, wisdom resides primarily at the top. In the open organization, on the other hand, a key belief is that wisdom is distributed among all the people in the company. This path requires a lot of courage, but it produces more avenues for creativity and innovation. Whereas the rank-based leader attempts to predict and control people and business conditions, peers in an open organization seek to cooperate, communicate, and evolve with people and business conditions by expanding internal networks of councils and task forces.

We have already examined in detail the assumptions, logic, and practices of peer-based thinking and how to build a peer-based organization. So we know what to expect in the open organization—the first form of a peer-based organization. Here you have management without hierarchy or rank, as peer councils are not subordinate to management, but rather mentored and coached by the senior executives. You also have hierarchy, but not one that subordinates the many to the few—it is a hierarchy of processes, projects, and assignments. In an open organization, councils are the multiple centers for decision making—the nodes of the organizational network. Executives and managers fill the role of cross-fertilizing ideas and best practices between councils, not as agents of top-down, command-and-control management, but as internal consultants—the connectors of the nodes in the organizational network.

When creating an open organization in a turbulent business environment, influence is superior to control. Control is about coercion — even coming from benevolent tyrants, it only brings compliance and dependence from employees. Power as influence, on the other hand, can bring commitment and interdependence. To exercise influence, the flow of information in the organization must be opened up through the creation of information-rich networks. This, of course, means allowing more open and honest communication about both business conditions and financial issues, greater equity of salaries and more aggressive rewards for innovation, and cross-fertilization of ideas and best practices in knowledge sharing. The simplest way to say it is that all members of the organization enjoy equal standing. Let's look again at some organizations from previous chapters that approximate open organizations.

W. L. Gore & Associates and Open Decision Making

An organization that has developed a similar philosophy and structure to the open organization is W. L. Gore & Associates, the company discussed in earlier chapters. Anyone interested in great companies should get to know this organization. Gore has approximately seven thousand employees, all called associates, in forty-five locations around the world. With revenues that top $1.4 billion, Gore is a very successful company.

Gore has dispensed with hierarchy; there are no "bosses" there. Instead, the company has developed a lattice structure that allows anyone to talk to anyone else in the organization without needing to go through any formal bureaucratic processes. The management philosophy closely resembles what I am presenting here. They have discovered the secret of both open information flow and managing through councils, and their continued profitability is evidence of the effectiveness of this approach. As Laird Harrison (2002) reported in *Time* magazine,

> *Each worker at Gore enjoys broad discretion to make minor decisions. Bigger ones—hiring and firing, setting compensation—are made by committees whose members constantly shift with the demands of business. Anyone can start a new project simply by persuading enough people to go along with the idea. Even Bob Gore, 64, chairman and son of the founders, has his compensation set by a committee.*

A prerequisite for being hired at Gore is to have an internal sponsor. This person then becomes the employee's mentor. Gore's management structure has no chain of command, but "leaders" chosen by peers, and any associate can take any idea or complaint to any other associate. Such a free-form structure is a great embodiment of peer-based thinking in an open organization.

Motek and Open Information

The absence of hierarchy at Motek allows decisions to be made closest to where the work is being done. Obviously this works most effectively when information is openly shared throughout the organization. Not surprisingly, in peer-based organizations sharing decision-making power and opening up the flow of information go hand in hand, and is a hallmark of an open organization like Motek. As mentioned in *Fortune Small Business* by one observer of Motek, Ellyn Spragins (2002), "Smart employees manage themselves perfectly well if they have complete information."

Orpheus Chamber Orchestra and Open Design

Orpheus realized early on that eliminating the command-and-control structure within which most businesses operate is risky. Getting rid of the orchestra's conductor could invite chaos! Most people have a difficult time imagining how to work without a leader because, for most of our human history, we have been organized in rank-based societies. To make the transition to peer-based organizations, peer-based thinking must be designed in. Orpheus realized this would require clear and unambiguous roles and responsibilities.

As presented in *Leadership Ensemble*, Orpheus designed organizational roles in a manner that would invite maximum participation in decision making. For each performance, Orpheus chooses a designated leader, not as a rank-based command-and-control figure, but as a facilitator to guide them through rehearsals and performances, following the Latin phrase *primes inter pares* ("first among equals"). This is not a permanent leadership position, but rather one that is changed at regular intervals to give others the opportunity to assume greater decision-making responsibilities.

Orpheus also chooses five to ten musicians to serve as the "core team," similar to a peer council, for each performance. Their role is to develop musical interpretations and ideas to improve each musical production. Other "committees" are also chartered at different times to make important decisions facing the orchestra. In each case, the design is intended to reduce rank-based thinking and foster peer collaboration. At Orpheus, each associate's priority is to use his or her talents to contribute to making the best possible musical product—leading is just another skill set associates develop, not a primary position they hold.

This peer-based design ensures that the primary focus of the organization is serving the customer and that each employee develops decision-making abilities that center on customer and other stakeholder needs. At Orpheus, the way organizational roles and responsibilities are designed to distribute power and authority to all members of the orchestra generates tremendous resiliency and innovation, not to mention spectacular musical performances.

From Open to Leaderless Organization

Through expanding decision-making freedom via peer councils, each person in an open organization finds opportunities to exercise "leadership." As this peer culture develops, employees are empowered to act without necessarily needing approval from higher-ups; in fact, the very term *higher-ups* doesn't make sense in the open organization, for there is no *higher*. It's a form of organizational decentralization in which no one entity or agent within the organization has complete command and control—power will naturally flow where it is most needed at the time.

It seems that the time will come in an open organization when even the advisory role of senior executive leaders will be a hindrance to successful decision making. Within fifty years we might be moving to the strange attractor of the leaderless organization. The exciting thing is that "leaders" do not need to control it. In fact, in many ways leaders are irrelevant to the inevitable development. Aristotle defined organisms as having within themselves their own possibility for development. Organisms do not require outside forces in order to grow and evolve. Organizations have within themselves this same power. They contain everything they need to open up the possibilities for development. They will grow into these possibilities without leaders or outside consultants. The strange attractor of the leaderless organization is the most exhilarating of these possibilities.

THE LEADERLESS ORGANIZATION

Peter Drucker (1988) has said that in today's business environment you cannot manage people in the traditional way. Knowledge workers are different and demand work that is more meaningful. In the future, we can expect even greater changes that will characterize the leaderless organization. Three essential differences distinguish the leaderless from the open organization.

- **Absence of professional managers and supervisors**. In the leaderless organization, managing is not a career, but rather a competency that everyone in the organization will be able to develop.

- **Task forces and peer councils extending across company boundaries**. In the leaderless organization, task forces and peer councils may not even be actual employees of the company. Given the needs of the market and demands of the business, the organization will determine the best way to meet customer needs. This will not require control, but influence on the various stages of the value creation chain. Thus, much work might be contracted or outsourced to organizations that have formed alliances with the leaderless organization.

- **Ability to stretch and fold in response to market conditions**. This ability makes the leaderless organization incredibly resilient. In today's turbulent business environment, with its high rate of energy circulation, companies must be able to deal with both tension-expanding (stretch) and tension-compressing (fold) forces. Leaderless organizations will be able to *stretch* to accommodate special needs and then return to shape or *fold* back. They will be able to deal with uncertainty by flexibly changing structure when necessary and then reconfiguring without breaking apart.

Let's look at each of these three characteristics of the leaderless organization in more detail.

Absence of Professional Managers and Supervisors

With his usual prescient insight, Drucker (1988) has seen the future of strange attractor organizations and the strange attractor economy. The whole meaning of organizations, Drucker argues, must change in consequence. He talks about the age-old search for the one right organization, and that there can no longer be any such thing as the one right organization. As we know, the "right" type of organization will depend on the business conditions, the level of energy and complexity in the business environment, and the wisdom and creativity of the individual peer-based organization.

In the strange attractor world of organizations in which leaderless companies will emerge, fierce competition between companies will coexist with a lot of collaboration. Despite the competition, there will be a free flow of ideas and people between companies. Employees will be counted as assets, and "leaders" will be counted as costs. In a leaderless organization, workers count, supervisors are obsolete. This does require a new gestalt for organizational thinking.

A leaderless organization will be characterized by an unequivocal and explicit rejection of the myth of leadership. It will operate with the assumption that employees are naturally motivated and interested in creating and distributing value to everyone who has a stake in the organization. Further, it will assume that everyone is capable of participating in decision making, and the arena of action will be networks of people learning and deciding together what to do next. Peer management wisdom will replace classical leadership as the norm that guides behavior. Councils and the cross-functional teams chartered by the councils will be the flexible centers of decision making in the leaderless organization.

The full implementation of peer management wisdom will see the demise of the concept of the executive as we have known it; organizations will not have room for the baggage of professional executives. It will include equalizing salaries and increasing monetary rewards for innovators within the company; increasing the flow of information through methods such as open book management; and increasing the sharing of knowledge between people in the organization. Designated executive "leaders" will be redundant, as power and decision-making responsibilities will have been spread throughout the company. Council membership will include employees of the organization, key customers, important vendors and suppliers, and perhaps even competitors. The task forces they charter to do the actual work may, or may not, be employees of the company.

Task Forces and Peer Councils Extending Across Company Boundaries

While organizations will be of various types and in different stages of development or decline, the evolution of the global marketplace itself is bringing us to the strange attractor of leaderless organizations. As boundaries dissolve and energy flows, artificial walls will fall—and any wall will be seen as artificial. Contemporary evolution theory teaches us that new species evolve away from the center, on the fringes. On the fringes of work and organizational life today, we are already beginning to see borderless organizations and workers.

Imagine: Employee A works for company B while simultaneously working on projects for companies C and D. As former and current rivals, companies B and D together redesign a key industry process to benefit all consumers. Company C brings employees and customers together on a team to work on a particular project, but when the project is completed, the team is disbanded and the team members go off to work on another team or even for a different company. Competing companies B, C, and D along with others in the industry meet together on a regular basis, not to collude and jack up prices, but to cooperate over shared resources, including workers, thereby lowering prices.

Further, as Art Kleiner suggests in *The Age of Heretics* (1996), "We can imagine a time when factories that make Fords on Monday make Chevrolets on Tuesday . . . and refrigerators on Wednesday. If such a time ever came to pass, economies of scale would be meaningless" (340). This is the strange business world of the strange attractor organization. In this world it will be difficult to distinguish companies as boundaries continually dissolve and the lines separating companies become blurred. Workers will move from project to project, from assignment to assignment, from organization to organization. Careers will be defined not by the company you work for, but by the work in which you specialize or generalize, given your unique combination of talents, strengths, and interests, or in other words, your own unique blend of intellectual capital.

In many cases, knowledge workers will not even be employees of the organization for which they work. Instead they will be contractors, experts, consultants, part-timers, joint venture partners, and so on who will identify themselves by their own knowledge rather than by the organizations that pay them. Boundaries between people and organizations will be seen to be illusionary and harmful as energy flow, degrees of freedom, and relationships become increasingly chaotic. Many, if not most, workers will essentially become independent contract workers.

Kleiner makes the following suggestions:

Some companies become more like banks, providing money to fund projects. Others evolve into contracting agencies, assembling teams of people to meet a particular need at will. Others find their real power comes from being distribution and trading systems. . . . Still others survive as purveyors, primarily, of a brand name. Everything else might be contracted out. (341)

This is what I believe could happen. When peer-based thinking becomes more common and as networks begin to dominate the corporate landscape, cross-functional councils and task forces will spin off from companies and become quasi-autonomous groups of skilled people who contract their services to different organizations or to different sources of financial capital. In spin-offs, the spun-off firm might still be owned by the original proprietors or just have key players from the original firm who brought along key intellectual capital or an important customer base. The original firm will maintain its mission and core competencies managed by the councils and the task forces they charter.

With the leaderless organization, we're also entering what Lester Thurow (1999) has called the free agency era of employment. This view of the future of employment is consistent with what many career specialists are predicting today. Individuals will begin to see themselves as independent contractors who will team with others and market themselves to businesses needing their services. Corporate cradle-to-grave job security is already a thing of the past. Now corporations are about to learn that just as business conditions no longer make long-term commitments to employees feasible, their employees will no longer be interested in a long-term relation with them. Instead, skilled workers are being attracted to a dynamic state of sequential contract work on different project teams for different companies.

High-tech entrepreneurs are already behaving this way. Several highly skilled individuals come together to create a product or service with the goal not of building a long-term business, but of becoming successful enough to attract attention and be bought out by a large company. The entrepreneurs then take their money, go their separate ways, and find their next project, thus creating ad hoc networks of relationships and complementary skills that can be reassembled in the future.

Some might be frightened by this picture of the near future, yet I see great freedom and opportunity. With this accelerated rate of energy flow comes almost limitless freedom, as boundaries evaporate and people regardless of income level, social status, race, or gender discover their options are only limited by their imagination. There will also be greater freedom and opportunities for organizations. Recall the "stretch" and "fold" properties of the strange attractor. At any one moment in the history of the dynamical system, two events or states are *folded* into close proximity, while in the very next moment they are *stretched* unpredictably far apart. This is due to the nearly infinite degrees of freedom possessed by the strange attractor system.

Ability to Stretch and Fold in Response to Market Conditions

In strange attractors the stretch and fold properties create universal and wonderful shapes that result from two antagonistic tendencies: to converge and to diverge. In strange attractor organizations this is accomplished through diversity. When diverse individuals are organized into networks, they are able to create highly adaptable and resilient forms. From moment to moment choices are made by the system that cannot be predicted, so paths are followed that cannot be foreseen. Yet, even if the moment-to-moment evolution cannot be known, nor the behavior of the parts be anticipated, the system as a whole is fully knowable and predictable.

Hierarchy is inadequate in this strange world; it will break apart under the stresses of uncertainty and turbulence. Companies need to develop the elasticity and the plasticity that is characteristic of the stretching and folding of the strange attractor! The leaderless organization is one that can thrive in a world of nomadic teams and redefine its identity to participate meaningfully and profitably in this new world without boundaries. This will be a world of less certainty but greater possibilities. The leaderless organization is perfect for this type of business environment.

By providing the central core of capital and other resources, yet contracting out the work flows to "nomadic" project teams, the leaderless organization is aptly suited to instantaneously respond to customer needs and stretch quickly in any direction the market moves while being able as well to fold back when business conditions require it. Surprisingly, the organizations who make this transition will find that order is for free, and increasing returns are the norm. It is a world, the strange attractor organization, where there are no losers, except those who refuse to participate. Everyone can win and no one need lose with the possibility of increasing returns.

One strategy touted today is to own as much of the value chain as you can. Why? To control it. But this is bad strategy and bad philosophy. You can't control it, but you will increase your costs and invite the demons of diminishing returns to torpedo your company. You don't need to own assets and infrastructure to generate revenue and profit streams. In the strange attractor world, power is understood to mean influence, not control. Spin-offs and alliances will be central in the shift from open to leaderless organizations.

A PriceWaterhouseCoopers study released in November 2000 showed that companies that made alliances experienced 20 percent more growth than those that did not. Strange attractor organizations will own less of the value chain, but influence more. Through alliances, outsourcing, independent contractors, and other means, leadership organizations will distribute the various aspects of the value chain around and sometimes own nothing more than the brand. This will open them up to increasing returns by requiring less cash, giving them greater flexibility and speed, and granting them access to the best minds in the industry. It will also spread out overhead costs in such a way that costs stay down so prices can stay down and salaries can go up.

Many Internet-based start-ups are already acting like the semi-autonomous teams of the strange attractor, or leaderless, organization. I know of several young entrepreneurs who have founded dot-com companies with a five-year plan in mind. They have no intention of building a long-term business, but only of putting together a team to do something phenomenal, attract the attention of an already established business, and within five years get bought out. They are behaving very much like the individuals who see themselves as independent contractors and team with others on a project-to-project basis. In many ways they are creating the pattern that most workers of the future will follow.

Of course the majority of dot-coms following this strategy have failed. Their downfall can be traced to the failure of dot-com leaders to manage the increased energy flow and implement appropriate managerial systems and processes—and the fact that the marketplace hasn't yet developed the infrastructure to handle this new type of company. While they were already acting like strange attractor teams, there were no strange attractor organizations to support them. In the future, when long-term businesses themselves have jumped into the strange attractor world, the infrastructure will be in place to support this new wave of project-based careers, and there will be very little risk in this type of employment. In fact, I believe it will be more secure than what many experience today.

Increasing Returns in Peer-Based Organizations

Consider the following: Currently, if you want to overnight a forty-page document from one coast to the other, with Federal Express it costs $16; with the U.S. Postal Service it costs $3. If you decide to fax the document, the cost is $9. However, if you decide to e-mail it, the cost is only 9 cents. Not only is e-mail the fastest way, it is also the cheapest. This development of progressively lower costs and higher benefits will be characteristic of leaderless organizations as less and less structure comes between the sender and the receiver of information.

As costs continue to decrease, the barriers for anyone entering the market go down as well, which lowers the cost even more.

Positive feedback produces increasing returns, whereas negative feedback produces diminishing returns. Where structure is minimum and energy flow is maximum, positive returns dominate and prediction and control are impossible. In the stability of the hierarchy, prediction, control, and command seem possible and desirable; but in the chaos of the strange attractor, unpredictability, cooperation, and communication are required. These are nonlinear traits and call for peer-based management techniques.

Conclusion

The attainment of the three essential characteristics of a leaderless organization—the absence of professional managers and supervisors, task forces and peer councils extending across company boundaries, and the ability to stretch and fold in response to market conditions— is hard to imagine for today's organizations. It will require the rejection of the myth of leadership and the practice of distributed decision making with peer-based thinking. In a leaderless organization, each person has his or her value and dignity honored, has a sense of responsibility for the common good, and has an equal opportunity to participate in decision making as well as equal access to information. Individuals make choices with open access to relevant information that will allow everyone an equal opportunity and the chance to become the architect of his or her own career.

Just like the strange attractor, the leaderless organization will be able to shape itself to whatever reality presents itself given the stretch and fold properties of the external networks it creates. In this phase of organizational life, it is not of decisive importance that any particular organization survive. It is the continuity of business and social processes, such as the production and distribution of goods and services, that must be maintained no matter which particular company does it.

This is a very hopeful view. As Philip Slater argues in his book *A Dream Deferred* (1992), democracy is inevitable, for it is the only social system capable of handling successfully the constantly accelerating rate of energy flow and complexity of our near future. In peer-based capitalism the arena of action will be networks of individuals leading and deciding together what to do next, where decisions are based on open systems and freely available information. Individuals will make choices that allow everybody equal opportunity and greater equality in distribution of the world's goods and services.

CONCLUDING THOUGHTS

Some look at things that are and ask why. I dream of things that never were and ask why not? —**George Bernard Shaw**

The recent and ongoing corporate scandals have led many of us to soul-searching and a reexamination of organizational leadership. Many companies do an incredible amount of harm to people and to our planet, thus adversely affecting future generations. In almost every organization, be it social, corporate, religious, or governmental, we observe those of a high financial or political rank—the organizational elites—taking advantage of their power and position to benefit themselves at the expense of those beneath them in the hierarchy. I have, however, a pervasive and enduring hope in our common human capacity for goodness; and I still believe that creating successful organizations is our best avenue for establishing global prosperity and peace. But we need to reconcile two contrasting positions: Are global corporations to be viewed as the great threat to future global prosperity, or as the great hope for future global prosperity? Whichever wins out—corruption and abuse of power or global peace and prosperity— I believe, will depend on the context we create for governing our organizations.

Unfortunately, as we have seen, the rank-based thinking of the myth of leadership creates an environment of low trust, lower morale, and even criminal activity, as determined by two principles: (1) genuine communication will occur only between equals and (2) secrecy breeds corruption and abuse of power. In any organization where inequality and secrecy dominate organizational life, lack of trust will be endemic, and even good people, eventually seduced by their privileges of rank, will abuse power. These principles hold in any organization, whether it is a family, a church, a government, or a corporation. The key is to know how to design organizations that recognize these two principles in order to create companies of peers where there are no secrets. That is the challenge I have addressed in this book—the challenge of creating peer-based organizations.

TIME TO REDEFINE OUR ORGANIZATIONAL LIFE

How we can instill work in any organization with purpose and joy and give members of each organization a sense of meaningful contribution to a greater community? How can we design our organizations so that the personal development of each member is just as important as exceeding profit expectations? The current concept of leadership, the

myth of leadership, is failing to do the job; only the peer-based organization will be successful. And the peer-based organization, as we
have seen, will eventually produce the leaderless organization.

But don't we need leaders? Doesn't someone have to be in charge?
These questions, and others like them, reveal both a positive intent as
well as some hidden assumptions. The hidden assumptions are simply
those of the rank-based myth of leadership. It is the mistaken belief
that only a select few individuals in any organization have either the
right or ability to monopolize power and control, to keep secrets and
restrict both information and participation in decision making. We are
all aware of the deleterious effects of this rank-based management system. The positive intent is, however, the realization that a management system is required. Certain management functions—setting
goals and objectives, scheduling work, marshaling resources, solving
problems—need to be performed. Many people imagine that these
duties can only be performed by a Big Chief or a hierarchical, rank-
based leader. I disagree. We have seen how these management functions can be performed in a leaderless organization through peer
councils and the practice of rotational leadership.

But isn't leadership important for an organization? Don't we need
strong leadership today? When we ask these questions, what we really
mean is that vision, wisdom, competence, communication, teamwork,
and similar attributes are important for an organization. What we fail
to recognize is that our concept and practice of the myth of leadership privilege an elite few and disadvantage the vast majority in a way
that works against and undermines those very attributes we desire. We
need wise people. We need visionary people. We need practical people. We need to be able to harvest the intelligence and strength of
every member of our organizations. We cannot afford to restrict decision making to a select, small few and ignore what philosopher
Michael Polanyi has called the tacit knowledge of the many.

The Transformation to a Peer-Based Organization

The core belief behind peer-based organizations is that every member of the organization, from the CEO to the front-line worker—albeit with different talents, ambitions, and contributions—has equal standing when it comes to information sharing and participation in decision making. The transformation to a peer-based organization needn't flow from the top down. I can envision a peer-based initiative within a single region or a few regions or departments of an organization; or even as a manager within his or her own small area. For instance, a typical manager, or team leader, can begin to apply the assumptions, logic, and practices of peer-based thinking. Through his or her mentoring, the team is successful, and the manager is promoted to run a larger venue, where he or she repeats the peer-based methods with the same success. Those left behind continue and others are promoted and spread peer-based thinking until large areas of the organization are applying these methods and experiencing this type of success.

Mapping Best Practices

One key aspect of peer-based thinking to touch on here is the mapping of best practices in the organization to discover the underlying normative pattern of recurrent operations; that is, uncover the implicit method. This doesn't mean copying from the procedures manual or even asking highly successful people to explain their approach, but observing them in action to see what they're actually doing. Most people's explanation of their behavior differs from what they actually do. This is because we all know more than we can say. Much of the intellectual capital in an organization consists of tacit knowledge. Because it is not captured, it is not teachable; and so this tacit knowledge is frequently lost by organizations.

When it is captured, best practices for all of the significant work in the organization can be methodically created and taught to others. In this way, the intellectual capital in a business can be turned into structural capital and become part of the long-term fabric of the organization. By uncovering the methods already operative within the organization, and not importing generic models from some self-interested consulting firm, the organization remains centered on its own authentic business identity. This mapping of implicit methods is facilitated when peer councils take over from rank-based managers, and senior executives stop being leaders and instead act as consultants to their people, who are now allowed to lead themselves.

Intellectual Skills Training

Another important practical aspect of peer-based thinking is training members of the organization in "hard" intellectual skills and not as much in "soft" emotional skills. It takes certain intellectual skills—creative thinking, critical judgment, the ability to build strong relationships, and so on—to be successful in dynamic organizations. These skills will become increasingly valuable. People in organizations need to be given the right training to be able to develop these intellectual skills and to prepare them for leaving the safety and comfort of hierarchy. They then can embrace the expanded degrees of freedom in the open organization and eventually thrive in the strange attractor environment of the leaderless organization. Typical soft skills training lacks method and is ineffective in dealing with the dynamic in organizations. It might very well be of some assistance in the life of the individual, but it will not affect the development of the organization.

Organizations and individuals must apply their own creativity and talent in defining themselves. This requires that managers trust their people with the creation and implementation of strategies, and to be able to identify and solve the problems facing the organization. This occurs when an organization adopts peer-based thinking, charters peer councils as the primary decision-making bodies, and abandons its infatuation with "heroic," rank-based leaders.

FROM LEADERS TO MENTORS AND EXEMPLARY LIVES

The terms *leader* and *leadership* carry around so much baggage in the form of the assumptions of the myth of leadership, that both need to be shelved for a while and neither used nor abused. We can admit that a leader's actions matter, that leaders can play an important role, and that not all leadership training is detrimental. But ultimately we need not heroes, but models of exemplary lives—what we all can achieve not by becoming like them, but by becoming our own unique selves. The many excellent new ideas in management thinking over the past two decades have been minimized by the absence of peer-based relationships. Only with the method of peer-based thinking can important disciplines, habits, and emotional intelligence come to full maturity.

Indeed, my own personal mission as an organizational consultant is to mentor organizations and individuals in becoming more healthy, meaningful, and prosperous. By *healthy*, I mean to become whole, complete, and dignified. By *meaningful*, I mean to experience joyful work and caring relationships. By *prosperous*, I mean to be profitable and economically secure. Designing, managing, and working in organizations should be a joyful thing. We are constantly re-creating our organizations. That's a fact, so how should it be done? I believe it will be through peer mentoring, not rank-based command and control, that both organizations and individuals can realize the strategic qualities of their "diamond strength": alignment, openness, transparency, and competence. They need to be aligned with their basic needs and desires. For individuals, this also implies that they must apply peer-based thinking at home as well. And they must maintain their integrity, stay teachable, be receptive to feedback, constantly learn, and work to discover their own strengths and weaknesses.

Peers don't need a leadership bureaucracy—they can together decide on issues and then implement their decisions. For the sake of efficiency, they may at times need to designate one of their members to be first among equals, as a facilitator of the process or coordinator of the decision implementation. And they will be more successful and prosperous than their rank-based rivals.

THE ORGANIC LIFE OF ORGANIZATIONS— SOME PREDICTIONS AND CHALLENGES

The evolution to the strange attractor of leaderless organizations is inevitable. The organic life of organizations does not require outside forces in order to grow and evolve. Organizations have within themselves the ability to grow and adapt to be successful in any environment. They will grow into these possibilities without leaders or outside consultants. One way or another, the limits of hierarchy will be transcended to yield a more exciting and abundant future for everyone.

The walls and boundaries that separate us will crumble as the ever-increasing flow of energy brings with it greater freedom and less structure. This will happen whether through our concerted, intelligent cooperation or against our will, but in accord with nature's continual push for renewal. Today, as the complexity and flow of information in world markets accelerates, we are witnessing the transition from ranking to linking in the network society. This is pulling organizations into another organization attractor and has opened up the need for peer-based organizational management to create the space for both the open and the leaderless organization.

The practice of peer wisdom will create the space for peer-based organizations to emerge without force or coercion. Indeed, this is how all natural life works; not from top-down decision making, but from bottom-up emergence. It's all about creating the right space through peer-based management for the appropriate organizational attractor to emerge.

The Challenge

We all spend the majority of our time in organizations—whether it is our family, our community, or our workplace—so it should be joyful. Fear and insecurity inhibit our ability to relinquish supposed control and power and become comfortable just letting go and cooperating. We are insecure because we feel that our survival is threatened by fast-paced change and the unknown. But our survival is not threatened— we can trust the dynamic that powers every complex system. Einstein asked whether this is a good universe or not—can the universe be trusted to be beneficial to human life? In a way, how a person answers that question will determine how he or she manages. This book answers that question strongly in the affirmative.

We must acknowledge the occasional brutality of business, but we should remember to celebrate its essential goodness, beauty, and variety. Each of us possesses remarkable talents to contribute toward the success of our organization, and we are naturally motivated to use our talents for something larger than ourselves. Yet, we are pilgrims in an unfinished universe. We are co-creators of our collective future. It should be a future we accomplish, not through coercion and force, but through the subtle influence of persuasion, cooperation, and joy.

REFERENCES

Barabási, Albert-László. 2002. *Linked: The New Science of Networks.* Cambridge, MA: Perseus.

Bohm, David. 1996. *On Dialogue.* New York: Routledge.

Briggs, John, and F. David Peat. 1989. *Turbulent Mirror.* New York: Harper & Row.

Byrne, John. 1999. "21 Ideas for the 21st Century." *Business Week,* August 30, cover story.

"The Capitalist Century." 2002. *Fortune,* March 6, F1–F97.

Carlyle, Thomas. 1966. *On Heroes, Hero-Worship, and the Heroic in History.* Lincoln: University of Nebraska Press.

Case, John. 1993. "A Company of Businesspeople." *Inc.* magazine (April): 79–93.

Castells, Manuel. 1996. *The Rise of the Network Society.* Vol. 1 of *The Information Age: Economy, Society, and Culture,* 3 vols. Cambridge, MA: Blackwell.

De Geus, Arie. 1997. *The Living Company.* Cambridge, MA: Harvard Business School Press.

Drucker, Peter. 1988. "The Coming of the New Organization." *Harvard Business Review* (January–February). Rpt. in *Knowledge Management.* Boston: Harvard Business School Press, 1998, 1–19.

Eliot, T. S. *Collected Poems, 1909–1962.* 1984. London: Harcourt Brace Jovanovich.

Flaubert, Gustave. 1949. *Madame Bovary.* 1856. New York: International Collectors Library.

Foucault, Michel. 1980. *Power/Knowledge: Selected Interviews and Other Writings, 1972–1977.* Ed. Colin Gordon. London: Harvester.

Gladwell, Malcolm. 2000. *The Tipping Point: How Little Things Can Make a Big Difference.* New York: Little, Brown & Co.

Gleick, James. 1988. *Chaos: Making a New Science*. New York: Penguin Books.

Greenleaf, Robert K. 1977. *Servant Leadership: A Journey into the Nature of Legitimate Power and Greatness*. New York: Paulist Press.

_____. 1996. *On Becoming a Servant Leader*. Ed. Don M. Frick and Larry C. Spears. San Francisco: Jossey-Bass.

Haire, Mason, and Willa Grunes. 1950. "Perceptual Defenses: Processes Protecting an Organized Perception of Another Personality." *Human Relations* (November).

Harrison, Laird. 2002. "We're All the Boss." *Time*, bonus section, "Inside Business." April 8.

Havel, Vaclav. 1994. *The Art of the Impossible: Politics As Morality in Practice*. New York: Fromm.

Hobbes, Thomas. 1982. *Leviathan*. 1651. New York: Viking Press.

Jennings, Jason. 2002. Letter. *USA Today*, November 22.

Kafka, Franz. 1981. *Franz Kafka Stories, 1904–1924*. London: MacDonald & Co.

Kleiner, Art. 1996. *The Age of Heretics: Heroes, Outlaws, and the Forerunners of Corporate Change*. New York: Currency Doubleday.

Klinger, Scott. 2001. "The Bigger They Come, the Harder They Fall: High CEO Pay and the Effect on Long-Term Stock Prices." April 6, http://FairEconomy.org//CEOPay.html.

Kuhn, Thomas. 1962. *The Structure of Scientific Revolutions*. Chicago: University of Chicago Press.

Lewin, Kurt, Ronald Lippett, and Ralph White. 1939. "Patterns of Aggressive Behavior in Experimentally Created Social Climates." *Journal of Social Psychology* 10: 271–301.

Lobell, John. 1985. *Between Silence and Light: Spirit in the Architecture of Louis I. Kahn*. Boston: Shambhala.

Milgram, Stanley. 1983. *Obedience to Authority: An Experimental View*. New York: HarperCollins.

Pascale, Richard, Mark Millemann, and Linda Gioja. 2000. *Surfing the Edge of Chaos: The Laws of Nature and the New Laws of Business*. New York: Crown Business.

Patton, George. 1949. *War As I Knew It*. Boston: Houghton Mifflin.

Porter, Michael E. 1996. "What Is Strategy?" *Harvard Business Review* (November–December): 61–78.

Robertson, James Oliver. 1980. *American Myth, American Reality*. New York: Hill & Wang.

Seifter, Harvey, and Peter Economy. 2001. *Leadership Ensemble: Lessons in Collaborative Management from the World's Only Conductorless Orchestra*. New York: Times Books.

Slater, Philip. 1992. *A Dream Deferred: America's Discontent and the Search for a New Democratic Ideal*. Boston: Beacon Press.

Spragins, Ellyn. 2002. "Motek: The Best Company to Work For Anywhere?" *Fortune Small Business*, October 21.

Stack, Jack, and Bo Burlingham. 2002. *A Stake in the Outcome: Building a Culture of Ownership for the Long-Term Success of Your Business*. New York: Currency.

Tainter, Joseph A. 1988. *The Collapse of Complex Societies*. Cambridge, MA: Cambridge University Press.

Taylor, Frederick W. 1942. *The Principles of Scientific Management*. 1911. New York: Harper & Bros.

Thurow, Lester. 1999. *Creating Wealth: The New Rules for Individuals, Companies, and Countries in the Knowledge-Based Economy*. New York: Nicholas Brealey.

Turban, Efraim, and Jay E. Aronson. 1997. *Decision Support Systems and Intelligent Systems*, 5th ed. Upper Saddle River, NJ: Prentice Hall.

Weisbord, Marvin R. 1991. *Productive Workplaces: Organizing and Managing for Dignity, Meaning, and Community*. San Francisco: Jossey-Bass.

Wheatley, Margaret. 1992. *Leadership and the New Science*. San Francisco: Berrett-Koehler.

Wilkinson, Richard. 1996. *Unhealthy Societies: The Afflictions of Inequality*. London: Routledge.

INDEX